James Lane Allen

Summer in Arcady

a tale of nature

James Lane Allen

Summer in Arcady
a tale of nature

ISBN/EAN: 9783742894342

Manufactured in Europe, USA, Canada, Australia, Japa

Cover: Foto ©ninafisch / pixelio.de

Manufactured and distributed by brebook publishing software (www.brebook.com)

James Lane Allen

Summer in Arcady

PREFACE

THIS preface is a flag of war, here run up and set freely waving on the breastworks of this story. If any timorous stranger, approaching it as an unknown fortress, should hesitate in foot and courage for lack of means to discover whether it were more prudent for him to advance or to retire, he will need but to glance up at these colours. They will acquaint him at once with the real nature of the forces entrenched behind; with the spiritual country to which they belong; with the cause they have undertaken to defend. Should the knowledge thus gotten, reveal to him his unexpected nearness to the border-land of a friendly power, he is invited to enter the fort, to study the low earthworks, to inspect the smallish garrison. But if he choose to consider himself confronted by a foe, he is free to depart whither he will, nor shall he be meanly fired upon as he turns his manly back.

Our separate, wholesome, altogether peaceful and rather unambitious world of books, lying far off to itself on this side of the ocean, has of late suffered a twofold invasion from the literature of the mother-country, that has well-nigh swept every living American author away before it. These two armies of invading volumes have had little in common but a port of departure and a port of entry; for while one has reached us as the forces of light — benign and always welcome — the other has spread abroad as the old and evil and ever-hated darkness. To those who understand, there is no need of plainer speech; to all others no need of speech at all. We know them too well — these black, chaotic books of the new fiction — know what unhealthy suggestions they have courted, what exposures of the eternally hidden they have coarsely made, what ideals of personal depravity they have scattered broadcast, what principles of social order they have attacked, what bases of universal decency they have been resolute to undermine. There is hardly a thing of value to the normal portion of the race, in its clean advance toward higher living, that they have not in effect belittled or insulted; there is scarce a thing that the long experience of the race has condemned and tried to cast off from itself as an element of decay, that they have not set upon with approval and recalled to favour.

It is against this downward-moving fiction of manifold disorder that the writer has ventured to advance a protest under cover of a story — a story, he is too well aware, that could not possibly carry with it the weight and measure of an opposing argument, but that should at least contain the taste and quality of healthful repudiation. To this end, and with the use of the weapons put into his hands, he has taken two robust young people in the crimson flush of the earliest summer of life; they are dangerously forefathered; they are carelessly reared; they are temptingly environed; they are alone with one another and with Nature; and Nature, intent on a single aim, directs all her power against their weakness. The writer has thus endeavoured to charge this story with as much peril as may be found in any of the others — even more; he has ventured to lay bare some of the veiled and sacred mysteries of life with no less frankness than they have used, but using, as he hopes, full and far greater reverence; and, nevertheless, from such a situation he has tried to wrest a moral victory for each of the characters, a victory for the old established order of civilized societies, and a victory for those forces of life that hold within themselves the only hope of the perpetuity of the race and the beauty of the world. Such and so far runs the plan and hoped-for mission of his work.

But furthermore: no man has ever sat gravely and sincerely down to study the lights and shadows of our common human destiny, desiring to transfer these in the due proportion of reality to the creations of his art, without sooner or later being driven to perceive that into nearly all the lights falls one dark ray from one great shadow,—the greatest shadow of the world, — its outcast women. This story has been sent very near to the old, old pathway that has always been trodden and is trodden to-day by these, alas! wandering, innumerable ones; and the writer has cast it in that direction with the utmost desire that it might do some good in this way:

If any mother should read this account of the life of a partly irresponsible girl, whose own mother had failed to warn her of the commonest dangers, had neglected to guard and guide her feet to the knowledge that may mean safety, it will haply arouse in her the question whether she herself is giving the needed warnings, throwing forth the proper guard, lending the upward guidance; for how much of the world's chief tragedy lives on and on for the simple lack of these?

If any father should read this story of temptation and struggle in two children, he might perhaps order his own life the better for having had the truth brought home to him, that whenever he weakens the moral fibre of his nature, he may be weakening as well not only the moral fibre of a son, but — what is far more terrible and pitiful in the judgment of the world — the moral fibre of his own daughter, yet unborn; for it is true that the fallen women of the race are in a measure set apart to that awful doom by the inherited immorality of their fathers.

If any girl, alone in the world, having no mother or counsellor of any kind, — alone with her youth, her innocence, her beauty, perhaps her poverty as well and the need of hard work, — not in the country chiefly, but rather in the vast city, in the treacherous town, — if any such poor, undefended child should chance to read this story, she should bear in mind that its main lesson and most solemn warning are addressed to her: the lesson not to trust herself, the warning to trust no other, without reservation — blindly led on by love; or else, sitting lonely in her sorrow on her bed at midnight, she may come to know what her countless sisters have known, — that even the purest love can do wrong, can betray, can be betrayed.

If many a man should read this story — married or unmarried, younger, older — who has resolutely set his feet in the pathway of right living, there is nothing here to tempt them thence; if they are straying elsewhither, there are some things here that might well follow after him, — if not with the power to recall, at least as a memory to rebuke; for he has found set forth in these pages the case of a boy, who, being greatly wronged by a past beyond his reach and associates beyond his control, nevertheless did struggle upward into something better than he had been, — so winning his happiness in one woman at last, as men must always win it, — by rising to it as something that stands above them, never going down to it as something that waits below.

SUMMER IN ARCADY

PRELUDE

SILENTLY summer waxes. The first wave of warmth trembles northward, pauses, flees back, is gone; but it has left an imperishable touch on thousands of delicate things as a glacier scars the rocks. Another wave, more heated, more vitalizing, creeps forward; even while advancing, it has died away amid the common chill. Then follow the sunlit breakers, running faster and farther toward the changeless coast of the North, until over the entire gentle zone settles one deep, tranquil, crystalline, perfumed sea.

Some day far out on this rockless ocean of air a solitary craft may be seen drifting — a gay little barge of two sails that seem woven of sunlight. From what port can it have started? Whither is it bound? What mariner holds it in charge? With what freight may it be laden for the good of the world? Turn your best glass upon it: you will never answer. No pilot stands on board; cargo there is none; of how it was built and where launched no hint is given; it changes its course at every point, and can be meant to reach no port at all: the most fragile and daring of earthly cruisers, careening fearfully to the one side or the other under the lightest breeze, like a yellow leaf on the slow winds of autumn.

By and by, in another part of the ocean, you observe a second vessel, fashioned like the first. Later, several; at last a fleet without number. No bay of the earth was ever so crowded with human sail. What can it mean — this warm sea of air crossed and recrossed at every parallel and meridian by rolling and rocking yellow-sail ships?

Two that have had naught to do with their own build and launch are drifting — far apart, unknown to each other. Borne nearer, some day they pass within signal range; but there is no salute: what do they care! Another day they crash into each other and are hard put to it to draw unharmed asunder; but they are not friends, they are not enemies: each steers calmly on. Before the summer is gone, however, and at the instant of Nature they come within hailing distance again. Now they rush together. The meeting of zephyrs could not be more soft; the onset of ironclads could not be more resolute. Out of that countless fleet they think of each other alone. To them the ages gone, the ages to come, are nothing; their one moment is eternity; the whole universe was created for the sake of their love. Eager, winnowing wings, built up so airily of a distant sunbeam and a few grains of dust! Weightless little bodies, heavy with Love! How they ride the blue billows of air, circling, pursuing, mounting higher and higher, the first above the second, the second above the first; then whirling downward again, and so ever fleeing and seeking, floating and clinging, blindly, helplessly, under the transport of all-compelling, unfathomable Nature!

As the end of it all, the two lash themselves together and go wandering by as one, or as one they come to stillness on the nearest blossom.

Not long afterwards the darkened, roughened sea of air is filled with another fleet — snow-flakes; and the wee yellow-sail ships of summer, where are they then?

Can you consider a field of butterflies and not think of the blindly wandering, blindly loving, quickly passing human race? Can you observe two young people at play on the meadows of Life and Love without seeing in them a pair of these brief moths of the sun?

I

THE warmth of June had settled over Kentucky, and yellow butterflies were thick along her path that day as Daphne crossed the sweet green fields.

She had not yet reached eighteen, and she was like the red-ripeness of early summer fruit where of late were white blossoms. A glance at her lithe, round figure, the unusual womanly development of which always attracted secret attention and caused her secret pain, could have made many a mother reflect upon the cruel haste with which Nature sometimes forces a child into maturity, and then adds to the peril of its life by covering it with alluring beauty.

Briskly she walked on, humming tunefully; now and then lifting her rustling, snow-white petticoats high over the sheep and cattle traces in her path, and watchful lest she be tripped and thrown. For the bluegrass and the tongue-grass and plantain and dog-fennel, growing along those byways that braid the rich meadows, soon mingle unless torn apart by passing feet; and she remembered that she was unfortunate about stumbling. So that her thoughts were wholly concerned with the safety of the small basket of eggs she was carrying.

Once she paused. A young farmer was singing in his field of corn not far away. It was a warm voice, pouring itself out in bold, glad unconcern of everything and everybody. She listened a moment, and then hurried on: neither the song nor the singer meant anything to her.

And nothing to Daphne, likewise, were the other wayside sights and sounds that morning. The eternal archway of blue, crossed by slow white clouds; the south wind playing with the hair on the back of her neck; the whole outlook of that green, quiet, sunlit land; plain, sturdy homesteads of brick lying about the horizon; motherly old orchards that had been the comfort of cellar and fireside for many a wintry year; fields of grain bending northward in long, shadowy, golden waves; red cattle grazing knee-deep on distant hillside pastures; the meadow about her set thick with violets and dandelions; the yellow-breasted lark springing up before her with a long silvery salute; the Kentucky warbler rising and falling through his low plane of feeding — these and the whole vast interwoven realm of Nature's influences were as nothing to her. And yet it was Nature that now drove Daphne swiftly onward along with orchard and cattle, grain, insect, and weed, to what we love pompously and ignorantly to call in human life the great hours of destiny.

II

The meadow was separated from the cornfield by a high staked-and-ridered fence. Along the fence at irregular intervals grew locust-trees—a familiar feature of the Kentucky fields. Had you climbed to the top rail and sat under the shade of one of these, as he often did, you would have seen coming down the corn-row toward you the young man, or boy, who had been singing.

He was in loose cowhide boots, into the tops of which he had stuffed his blue cotton trousers; his white cotton shirt was opened down the bosom, so that the cool breeze might blow in and keep him cool. It blew in now, showing his deep, clean, beautiful chest, and causing the shirt to bend out from his broad, flat back like a little bellying sail. His shirt and trousers were girt tightly about his waist; around his neck he had tied a handkerchief with a pink border;

and set well forward over his clear, careless eyes was a broad-brimmed hat of coarse straw, with a hole in the crown. A heavy-limbed, heavy-built, handsome young fellow of about nineteen, with a yellowish mustache just fairly out on a full red lip that had long been impatient for it.

The old horse kept his gait up and down the rows as evenly as though urged along by the pressure of steam; it would have been as likely for an alarm whistle to have blown off through one of his ears as for him to have stepped by mistake on a hill of corn; the corn itself was still too young for him to bite and so need a watchful curb; the share parted the furrow through a soil without clods or stones to roll over on the brittle shoots; so that with one hand lightly guiding the plough handle and the noose of his plough-line around his other wrist, what was there to keep the boy from singing? And of what should he sing at nineteen, in the month of June, with the gold of the sun on his face and its flame in his blood?

Once, as he reached the edge of the field

and swung his plough from the furrow into the next, he caught sight of a blue figure moving away along the meadow path. He dropped everything, and stepping over to the fence, leaned heavily and lazily upon it, watching in dead silence. To his gross instincts anything in the shape of a woman was worth gazing after, even at long range, — especially a woman alone. But beyond this passion his face betrayed no interest. The blue figure became smaller, bearing away with it through the quivering heat the fragrance and freshness of a hyacinth, and he returned to his plough and to his singing.

III

Daphne stepped out into the front porch of her father's house near ten o'clock the next morning with the empty basket in her hand: it gave her a pretext to go back to her aunt's; and to Daphne on this day anything was better than staying at home.

The houses were about a mile and a half apart as a crow flies. They were connected by a carriage and wagon road and by a foot-path; and even before Daphne was born this foot-path had become a little highway for the passage of creams and jellies, butter, fruit, vegetables, and the thousand more things, eatable, wearable, or otherwise usable that may be sent to and fro between friendly households in a remote country neighbourhood.

From childhood one house had been as nearly her home as the other. She had moved contentedly backward and forward between them, much as a pith-ball between two batteries; which, on being made negative, returns to be made positive; and having become positive, returns to be made negative again; and so on endlessly.

But during the last year or two, for reasons of which she knew nothing but of which Nature could have given a reasonable account, the pith-ball had begun to be jerked about in the most violent, irregular manner, under disturbances from another quarter, and the two batteries no longer held it in rhythmic peace: the child had become a woman, and there was no longer any one in either household to make her happy.

Some evidence of this complete discontent could have been gathered from the manner in which she had now paused on the steps of the porch, undecided whether to go or not, and looking with disapproval at the green landscape quivering with crystal heat.

The little brown porch had large white pillars, and over these had been trained a queen-of-the-prairie rose-bush. This hung heavy with bloom now, and there was the sound of droning inside the petals. Two bees rolled angrily out of a rose just over her head and she started aside; then going down the steps to an old calycanthus-bush of rare sweetness, she gathered several half-blown buds, and putting them into her bosom passed dreamily out of the yard.

She crossed the stable lot, full of dog-fennel and June-bugs, where the short-horn calves stayed, — her father made a specialty of young steers, — passed through a woodland pasture where the short-horn cows stayed, and began to cross a meadow where there were Southdown sheep.

If you can imagine a pond as growing to hate its smooth surface and wishing that the ducks and geese would all come wabbling down the hill, — a pond so lonesome in its way that it would be thankful for a few frogs at nightfall, — you will understand Daphne's state of mind as she strolled across the meadow swinging in both hands the basket to which she gave idle, vicious little kicks with her knees. Nothing better in the way of pleasure was within her reach than to have gone back to the calf-lot, caught a June-bug in the dog-fennel, and tied a thread to its leg merely for the excitement of hearing it buzz around, and of dodging when it darted at her with its prickly feet.

But to be satisfied with insects was not for such as Daphne. Once she did stoop down in the path to look closely at a most gorgeous dot of moving scarlet; and becoming interested, pulled a plantain and let the insect crawl on it and studied it. Her eyes were ravished with its splendour. A robe like that perhaps no queen had ever worn. What was the use of making such a thing so beautiful? And what was it doing in this big meadow all by itself? Daphne's thoughts on human life were not of a kind to have filled the note-book of Epictetus, or made Solon walk the floor for envy; but as she threw it away with a sigh she asked herself one mighty question: Why, in a world so full of people, should *she* be crossing the meadow without a companion?

Look to the right or to the left, only two things gave the slightest relief to her green world of loneliness: on one side the sheep; on the other the figure of the young farmer whose land adjoined her father's. He was resting on the top rail of the fence under a locust-tree, and was watching her with his hat in his hand; and once, as she looked that way, he put it on and took it off again with a movement that said "good morning," —said it with cordial good-nature. All at once, full of cordial, gay good-nature herself, Daphne took off her hat and waved it in return, laughing because she felt that he must be laughing also; and immediately the world became a different sort of place in which something does happen. The next time she looked at him he waved his handkerchief— it was pretty wet; so that Daphne drew out her fresh handkerchief from beneath her belt and waved it. Then he put his hands up to his mouth in the shape of a conch and shouted several words to her. She called back that she could not hear. He shouted again. And she again. Then he again. Then she no more; but with a gesture of impatience she pursued her way.

But she wished that she had heard. He had tried very hard to make her hear. And she looked again, thinking that if he cared to come across and walk beside her, and tell her, she would wait for him. But he had gone back to his work.

"Are you going to the picnic?"

This was all that he had said; and as he started down the corn-row, he whacked the old horse with the plough-line in a growing hope that he would meet her there.

IV

Daphne was kept at home during the next two days, with helping her mother make cherry preserves; and on the third day they had a roll for their twelve-o'clock dinner which would be the last of the season. After dinner she started to take a slice of it to her grandmother.

When she entered the meadow this time, she looked eagerly toward the row of locust-trees. There were seven of them from one end of the field to the other, and not a man under any tree. She began to feel fretful and sorry that she had come, and all at once she remembered how she hated to see her grandmother eat anything soft with her dry, withered, nimble little mouth. And then riding down the path toward her she saw Hilary, sitting sideways on the back of his horse.

He was returning from his dinner, and he was crossing the upper edge of the meadow to a pair of bars which opened into his field. But his roving eyes had lighted upon her, and with the idea of talking to her about the picnic he had turned his horse's head into the path. And since the old horse crept sleepily along in one direction and the child, now very wide awake, moved straight on in the other, they presently came together, nose to nose.

"You needn't pretend that you don't see me!" cried Daphne. She was radiant and laughing.

"I'm not looking at you, am I?" He had not turned his head.

"Very well; you needn't look. But get out of the path."

"*I*'m not in the path."

Daphne put her plate down resolvedly on the grass, closed her parasol, rested her hand on the horse's nose, tipped off his hat, picked it up and sent it whirling through the air, and taking her dumpling, sailed round him in triumph. She was greatly pleased with what she had done. In secret she was even more pleased with what he had done.

She heard his low laughter behind her, musical with good-nature, and she turned quickly and laughed back.

"Ah, ha!" she cried. "That's what you get for your impudence."

"Yes," he said lazily, after looking at her for a moment, "and what ought you to get for yours?"

He leaned over toward her, resting his elbows on the broad, fat back of the horse, with his chin in his palms. The sunlight fell on his yellowish hair and on his strong, bronzed face and neck; and his whole outstretched body lay basking as restfully as though asleep on a silvery white rug. She stood with a blue parasol on her shoulder, as though a strip of the lovely vault above had come down and arched itself over her head. Its shadow brought out the whiteness of her clear, firm skin, now moist with heat, the peony-like flush of her cheeks, the chestnut brown of her soft, thick hair, braided in two long plaits down her back. Her fresh lips parted slightly from her teeth like a crimson bow. Her bosom was rising and falling with her quickened breath. The warm odour of calycanthus buds stole outward. In all that Nature could do she was a challenge. His nostrils quivered, he slowly stretched his limbs, and his eyes filled with something warmer than sunlight.

"And what ought you to get for yours?" he repeated. Then sitting up, he called to her keenly:

"Stand still, Daphne! There's a bee coming to sting you."

One day when a child, up in the garret where she kept her china, Daphne had espied a gray object that looked a little like a honeycomb and a little like a spider-web, and she had put up an inquiring hand and pulled down a hornet's nest. There is apt to be a point about such things that keeps them remembered.

She now raised her shoulders to the back

of her neck, shut her eyes, and drew her scarlet lips apart.

"Quick!" she cried. "Kill it!"

He slipped down and kissed her, — not very quickly, — snatched her hat and was up again.

"You can open your eyes," he said quietly. "The bee's gone."

They were open — wide open — and the breath was all but out of her body.

He had put her hat on one side of his head and was laughing down at her in an unconcerned way, except for a look of roguish mischief. There passed through her mind like a scorching flash the remembrance of what she had heard about his ways with girls, and the colour began to leave her face. She could not even say, "How dare you!" He had dared so often already. That point seemed settled.

"Give me my hat," she said instinctively.

He nodded toward his, lying far out on the grass.

"You go pick up mine," he replied, laughing.

She did not know that the vines and leaves of her hat brought out in his head and face a likeness to Bacchus; but its influence drew her: it was daring, dangerous, rudely beautiful with the warmth of earth and vine and sun; and she cried out with a new pain in her anger:

"How dare you try to kiss me as you do other girls?"

"I don't kiss other girls," he answered, laughing carelessly just as before. "Only you."

With the instinct that prompts women when excited to put their hands to their hearts, she was pressing the tilted plate against her bosom, and the sauce had begun to trickle down the front of her dress.

"Look at you there!" he cried. "Don't waste that sauce."

When she glanced down and saw what had happened, the indignities and misfortunes of the occasion were too much for her reckless, passionate temper; and gathering herself up for a mighty effort, she pitched the dumpling at his head. He dodged, but some of the flying sauce struck his cheek; it glistened as though coated with gum arabic.

"Look at you!" he shouted again, "a-spoiling my clean shirt and a-gorming me up like a baby."

But Daphne was on her way home, bareheaded, defeated, and full of the further irritation that comes from sticky garments.

When she had gone about twenty paces, he called after her:

"Here's your parasol."

She walked on.

"Here's your hat."

She took no heed.

"Here's your dumpling."

Daphne would not have laughed for the world.

"Here's pretty much everything."

Daphne answered with two or three tears, and put up one hand to shield her eyes from the glare of the sun.

"You'll get sunstruck if you walk home that way."

There was a change in his voice, and she noted it. She put up both hands.

"I'll bring you your parasol if you'll say, 'Please, Marster.'"

Daphne now saw unexpected victory ahead. She took out her handkerchief and made a little white sunshade of it — with many signs of how hard a thing it was to do.

"Good-by!" His voice came with increasing penitence.

The end was nigh and Daphne was resolved that he must not see she had been crying: she took down the white umbrella and secretly wiped her eyes.

"Hello! Hold on there! Where are you going?" He was in dead earnest now.

Daphne thought to herself that she had managed this very well.

There followed a minute of silence and then she heard him say, "Get up, here!" and heard the old horse groan aloud at being kicked on both sides for no earthly reason known to him. Then behind her, getting louder and louder, she heard the rattle of the hames and the jangle of the trace chains.

Like many another woman, she felt that she must appear a terrible being in the presence of the man she had conquered. He must be made to realize what a vast power he had feebly attacked. But like many another woman, she was in doubt as to the terms on which she meant finally to make peace and as to the amount of her war debt. And then, human nature, while it knows how to act when wronged in one particular, becomes confused when offended in several — being much like a crow that can count one or two, but gets dreadfully puzzled over five or six. So many things had happened to Daphne that she was not sure how to itemize her indignation. Under the circumstances, instinct told her that it would be better not to say anything at all — that a stubbornly silent, angry-looking woman is a power hard to reckon with.

"Are you mad?"

He had jumped off the horse and was

walking in the grass beside her, and looking round into her face, bareheaded, smiling.

She made him no answer.

"I couldn't help it, Daphne. It wasn't the first time, you know; and I had never forgotten. How could I forget?" His tone was very gentle and apologetic and affectionate.

Daphne remembered instantly that once in a game of thimble, when it had been his turn to do the kneeling and the bowing and the kissing, he had kissed her; for no other reason really than that she was the nearest girl to him and he had not then lost his bashfulness. But such speeches have their effect. Daphne reduced her war debt one-half.

"We are no longer children," she remarked with dignity.

"That's all the more reason I couldn't resist," he replied insinuatingly.

"Say you are not mad," he added, as she made no further reply.

She gave him one look to show him how angry she was.

"I knew you were not mad," he cried, reading her through and through, and bursting into a laugh.

Daphne now began to get angry in earnest, and he saw it.

"Very well, then," he said, "I'm going to stay with you till you get in a good humour again."

He raised the parasol and held it over her. The plate was in his other hand and her hat dangled from his elbow. And then in a gay undertone, as if wholly to himself, he began to sing:

"O, there was a little boy who worked in the corn,
　　And a little girl who played in the hay;
　And he was alone and she was alone.
　　O, they lived to see their wedding-day.

"O, the little boy cried: 'Come play in my corn!'
　　But the little girl she cried: 'Nay!'
　And he worked on and she played on.
　　O, they lived to see their wedding-day."

He stopped singing and thrust his face around in front of hers again, with an inquiring smile. But he got no smile from her, so he went on:

"O, the little girl cried: 'I'm afraid of your corn!
    So you come play in my hay!'
The little boy sped but the little girl fled.
    O, he caught her on their wedding-day.

"O, all of you little boys out in the corn,
    And you little girls out in the hay,
May you play and work together in the right kind
    of weather.
    O, may you see your wedding-day!"

They had reached the meadow bars as he finished. He stopped abruptly.

"Here are your things," he said, handing them to her with quiet authority. "I must go back to my work now. Good-by! Be sure to be at the picnic," he added kindly as he turned away.

She stood rooted to the spot and watched him as he went back to his horse and rode away sidewise through the sunlight, singing, and without once glancing back at her. Then she started home, wounded and excited as she had never been.

V

In Kentucky June is the season for picnics in the woodland pastures. The skies are fairest then. The earth has the perfect beauty of the young summer. The big oaks and walnuts and maples cast their round shade heavy with new leaves. The breezes blow sweet with the scent of fields never far away, sweet with the odour of crushed grass. The warm-eyed, bronzed, foot-stamping young bucks forsake their plough-shares in the green rows, their reapers among the yellow beards; and the bouncing, laughing, round-breasted girls arrange their ribbons and their vows. It is the Arcady of that passionate land and people. It is the country dance of merry England, full of love and mischief, that was danced by our forefathers centuries ago, is danced to-day on Kentish greens, and is destined to be danced for hundreds of years to come among these unchanging Southern children of the mother-land.

That June Nature appeared in a dream to a young farmer of the neighbourhood. The next day he rode up the turnpike and down the lane, inviting everybody to his picnic. But Nature really issued the invitations. She said to the young women: "The young men will be there — that is all you need to know;" and to the young men: "The young women will be there — and that is all you need to know." And then she reflected further within herself: "These blindfolded children! They think they are giving a picnic: they do not see that it is mine. They do not look around them and behold with terror how I have called back to me nearly all their grandfathers and grandmothers; that I am about done with their fathers and mothers; and that their whole land — these rich old homesteads, these fields with herds and flocks, these crops, and orchards, and gardens — would soon become a waste unless I gave picnics and the like, from which I always gather fresh generations and keep things going. *I* will be at this picnic."

The morning of the dance came. The dew was hardly off the grass when into the woods hurried the young bucks on horseback, or in their new, or newly washed, buggies, with their radiant partners. But there were rockaways also with other girls sitting beside their mamas — those mamas who know how to take occasion by the foretop and who help Nature wonderfully with the origin of man.

Down the lane, not far away, the ring of a hammer ceased, and the negro blacksmith, having washed his hands and arms in the huge tub where he cooled his irons, locked the smithy door. Horse and mare and colt were to go unshod that day. They set a table under a sugar-tree, set a chair on the table, set the fiddler in the chair, set a pitcher of ice-water at his feet, and told him to strike while the iron was hot. He took a long, deep, contemptuous draught, struck a shower of musical sparks from his fiddle, hitched his chair so as to face a rectangular space where the sod had been removed and sawdust sprinkled, fixed his eye on the roof of green boughs covering it, and became lost to all further companionship with the human race.

"Go it, my children!" said Nature, looking on. "Dance away! Whatever is natural is right."

"Yes," said the Devil, who also attends picnics. "Go it, *my* children! Whatever is natural is right."

VI

DAPHNE awoke that morning with the dawn and the birds and the thought of the picnic. After breakfast, as he was leaving the house, she found courage to ask her father to let her go. He refused; he was an elder in the church, she a member. It was no place for her.

All the forenoon she sat in the front porch — near the droning of bees in the honeysuckles and the roses, looking across the bright fields toward the dark domes on the horizon under which she knew they were dancing. Once she slipped off in the direction of her aunt's. When she came to the meadow bars where two days before she had seen him riding away, she looked across at the locust-trees. No one was sitting there. She bent her ear, listening. No one was singing in the corn-field. How unutterably deserted and silent the earth was! Very slowly she went back to the porch and sat there.

Little things often determine the future of a girl, as the push of a finger will start a great rock down a mountain with ruin to everything in its path. During those hours Daphne took account of her life as never before, and the account consisted mainly of the things she had against her father. There were days when she hated him: this was one.

Two heroic necessities make up a large part of our life: to be made to do what we dislike, and to be withheld from doing what we desire. Early in childhood, Daphne's spirit had been broken to the first. No day passed without unpleasant duties; but these were so many burdens originating outside her own nature and laid upon her by those she loved; and for the bearing of other people's burdens, she had quick, warm sympathies, and would in time, perhaps, come to have the true womanly endurance. But life had no power of teaching her submission to the second of these hardships. The older she grew, the more passionate became her rebellion at ever being thwarted. Whenever she could not have her own way altogether, she always went as far as possible toward the forbidden. And of the things that had been forbidden her in the whole course of her life, nothing had ever been so hard as the command to stay away from this picnic. The desire to be there smouldered in her like a fire.

When her father came home at noon, she asked him again more boldly. He refused rudely; and after dinner, taking a pillow, he stretched himself on the long, green bench in the front porch, and told her to get the fine-tooth comb. It had been one of her duties when a little girl to be made to put him to sleep by combing the dandruff out of his hair while she was nearly dead for sleep herself. Sometimes her tears fell softly on his locks, and trickling over his brow had been understood by him as indications of his temperature. At other times she would deal him a fierce dig with the comb that awoke him with a tremendous wince and snort.

But to-day she combed her father's hair with

the softness women sometimes have that is so terrible to watch; and the soft movement of her magnetic fingers about his temples put him quickly to sleep. Then Daphne crossed her hands in her lap and simply looked at him. He might well have had bad dreams.

His nap over, as he was riding away from the stiles, he called to her carelessly to take the boys over to the picnic for a little while: *they* wanted to go.

It was the middle of the afternoon, then, when into the woods rattled an old rockaway, driven by a little bareheaded negro with a pea-stick for a whip. Beside him sat two white boys smaller still, and on the seat behind sat Daphne.

She had the negro drive to a distant fence-corner and got out unnoticed. When she approached the vehicles drawn up around the dancers, she searched until she found one that was vacant, and getting into it let the children go. They sped back to a hogshead of lemonade, which they had passed on the way, with a tin cup hanging low on the outside from a twine string, and she was left alone.

For a few minutes longer she indulged her angry, bitter thoughts against her father. He had a good buggy for himself; he was more than able to buy a new rockaway; instead, he made them keep on using the old one, which he varnished thickly over once a year at fair time. It rattled so loud on the turnpike that people could tell what was coming long before they could see what it was; and if she could help, she would never go to town in it except on rainy days when the spokes and hubs were swollen, and she could let down the side-curtains and sit far back inside. It was very dry weather now, however, and when they had turned out on the pike, and the little negro with a tremendous whack from his pea-stick had set things in violent motion, the sudden uproar — the mortification of having to go to the picnic in a sort of loosely jointed flying-machine — had brought back the feelings with which she had been struggling all day.

The rockaway in which Daphne, with Kentucky frankness, had now taken her seat and sat pouting was new and stylish. It made her feel respectable; and she might have been happier still if the family flying-machine, hidden behind the briers, could have caught fire from the trench near by in which they had barbecued the mutton, and been carried off as sparks and smoke. She could now receive without mortification the attentions of the young men of her acquaintance who did not dance on account of being members of the church; and Daphne knew also that it was not an unheard-of thing in a young man who did dance to prefer to sit with a girl in such an advantageous place.

Still, it was only in a half-hearted way that she brightened up and began to talk to the people of the neighbourhood in their carriages near her.

A middle-aged mother with a screaming baby in her arms got out of her carriage just ahead and hurried toward the rear. She caught sight of Daphne and called to her:

"*You* here! Tell your father to look out for his black sheep — Hilary's been dancing."

Hilary dancing! And now her father would have him up before the church! By and by the mother repassed.

"Whom has he been dancing with?" asked Daphne, in a voice faint and cold.

"With all the girls. Don't sit back here; you can't see. Come, get into my carriage."

"Thank you! I am going home soon," said Daphne. "I only came to bring the children for a while."

One of her little brothers now ran alongside the rockaway, and pointing to her called to some one behind:

"Here she is — in here."

Hilary came round eagerly.

"Well!" he said, with an air of tremendous relief, "why didn't you come over here sooner? I've been looking for you all day."

His chiding friendliness was so sincere that she let her hand lie in his with a sense of refuge. He wore his Sunday clothes; and he stood wiping his forehead and fanning himself with his new summer hat. A big spray of withered honeysuckle was in his buttonhole. His collar had wilted, and his flowing blue cravat was loose at his neck. His face had in it all the riotous passion of the earth and the sun at play.

"Why didn't you come?" he repeated in the tone of a good-natured scolding.

"I couldn't." Her lips began to quiver and her eyes fell.

"Well, it's not too late!" he cried, cheering her up roughly. "Come on and dance with me! They are just making up a set. Come on!"

He opened the door of the rockaway.

"Come on!" he repeated with overbearing confidence. "I want to dance with *you!*"

With a sudden thought Daphne's lips ceased quivering and her eyes flashed; a woman does not need more than a minute in which to revenge herself for a day or for a lifetime.

She put her daintily-slippered foot out on the step of the rockaway, and gave him her hands with a little laugh that was as reckless with joy as the note of an escaped bird.

When the dance was over they went back to the rockaway, happy and fanning themselves. As she resumed her seat she made way for him to sit beside her.

"Good-by!" he said with a gay dismissal, and without offering his hand, as he hurried off.

It was like a blow in her face. With a startled, yearning look at him, she sank miserably back into the corner.

For more than an hour she waited, but he did not come again; and toward dusk, having found her brothers, Daphne took each by the hand and started toward the rockaway.

As she was passing through the vehicles she heard his low, confidential talk close to her ear. The back curtain of a buggy was rolled up, and she saw his arm around a girl.

Soon a miscellaneous clatter arose on the turnpike and died away in the distance, leaving a mournful, white dust behind.

VII

WHAT are little brothers, if not spies and talebearers and jackals generally? Daphne's, on reaching home, ran confidingly to their father. That night the family were called into the parlour. Her father sat upon her case as a court of ecclesiastical inquiry; and at the neighbourhood church the next morning, which was Sunday, Daphne acknowledged her waywardness before the whole congregation, and was kept within the membership. Her sobs were accepted as showing the sincerity of her repentance; but only Daphne herself knew why they brought no relief to an unutterable heartache. Not that she did not believe that she had committed a sin; her religious training convicted her of this. For Daphne's idea of the devil was that he lived somewhere in the earth — perhaps moved about under her father's farm — and that he was altogether too near to be trifled with. To her mind he was especially on the lookout for young people who moved their feet in certain ways to the sound of music. If you can imagine a small insect on the outside of a walnut keeping quiet through terror of an enormous insect mysteriously at work on the inside, and reported capable of bursting through the shell if in any way annoyed, you will understand how grateful she was for now being given a chance to assure Beelzebub that she would never dance again.

But Hilary stood his ground — even though the devil's own. He was not at church that morning, having gone off in his buggy with a girl to another church miles away across the country; but he was quoted as having said that if the devil wanted him for dancing with the pretty girls at a picnic, he could have him — and welcome. But meantime, till he came for his property, he'd dance on.

Having twice gone to see him at his home without finding him, one afternoon during the week the elders of the church mounted their fat saddle horses and racked comfortably over to where he was ploughing on the other side of his farm. He was pouring out the everlasting praises of his favourite theme as they approached him down the corn-rows; and although their memories were now an armoury of scriptural texts, they might as well have gone out to capture a tremendous young bear by merely carrying along the sacred description of a rifle.

In neighbourhoods quiet and settled, everybody knows not only what kind of children are born in it, but what kind are going to be born; and a young man may gain a reputation before he earns it. Some quality in the strain of the family, or some sign in the early build and look of the boy himself, is held for as good or as bad as conduct; and old people, who may be stupid enough on other subjects, often scan their own offspring and that of their acquaintances with a preternatural wisdom in reading the early preparation of nature, and get ready in mind and heart, sometimes in distress, for what is sure to come in the course of time. And sometimes they scan them with as preternatural a folly.

Neighbourly talk had always greatly portended that in Hilary's case the boy would be father to the man; and the boy had always passed for what people who are more or less wooden, deem wild. The old stumps in a forest are wiser: they never reproach the dancing, sappy, leafy boughs.

In addition to these prophecies, his father had died before he turned eighteen; and at the period of passing into the years that nature makes so unruly, he had stepped forward to the head of the family and management of the farm. His middle-aged neighbours had then been forced to adjust themselves to a further change in his habits and his bearing, and it had gone hard with some of them; for the old are often shocked by the discovery that the young have grown up and must be treated as men. And he soon made them feel not only that he was a man, but that he had taken the bit entirely in his own teeth and meant to choose his own road and go his own gait.

It had come as a surprise, therefore, when the summer preceding this he had joined the church. His confession had been received at the time with secret misgivings: with misgivings they had seen him baptized, and with misgivings on the following Sunday morning they had presented him with a little red Testament as his earthly rule of faith and practice. But the entire congregation had filed past him, singing and offering him the right hand of their Christian fellowship, — some at least with that grasp of the hand which means forgiveness of the past, and the hope of a life where none of us shall need to be forgiven.

And now, in the first year of his membership, he had fallen from grace.

When the boy saw them coming toward him down the corn-rows, he laughed quietly to himself, stopped his horse, sat down on his plough, and began trimming his finger-nails; and the elders on coming up threw their legs over the pommels of their soft saddles and sternly whittled the butt ends of their switches as they reasoned with him touching his eternal damnation.

"No, sir," he said, at a certain point in the discussion, looking up at Daphne's father from under his old straw hat. "I can't honestly say to the church that I am sorry for what I've done, because I don't honestly believe that I've done anything wrong. All I am sorry for is that anybody else thinks so."

They had never talked with him seriously on any subject before. The cool, polite way in which he opposed his convictions to theirs as though they were entitled to equal respect left them ill at ease and they did not reply to his last words at once. He went on in a vein of gruff philosophizing:

"I come of a dancing family. Back in the wilderness, in the forts and cabins, they were dancing when they were not fighting, and fighting when they were not dancing. They were dancing in Virginia before they came to Kentucky. They were dancing in England before they came to Virginia. They were dancing wherever they were before that. I suppose they've been dancing since they were first created. I don't know much history, but I know a little. It's natural for people to dance. It does them good. I know it does *me* good."

Daphne's father made his one stern, brief rejoinder:

"You know the rule of the church?"

"But the church is wrong!" replied the young fellow, with a heavy, bludgeon-like handling of such ideas as he had. "It was wrong to take this position at the start. It will have to change. It is changing — already. In some parts of the country they don't turn the members out for dancing now. You know that. And you know that some of the best preachers in the church never have believed it a sin. There's a difference of opinion even in the churches. Then why don't you let me have my opinion? The greater part of the world agree with me. You have no more right to keep me from dancing than I have the right to make you dance — and I never would think of doing that."

"Brother Hilary," said the other elder, who was the kinder soul of the two, "don't you remember what the New Testament says about the eating of meat?"

"Yes," he replied, "but I don't think it means that I mustn't dance if you think it's wrong."

"That's just what it does mean," interposed Daphne's father. "*I* understand the Apostle."

"So do *I* understand him!" exclaimed the boy, giving a contemptuous cut at his boot-top with the end of his plough-line.

"Beware of causing others to stumble," said the milder officer, who hereupon shut up his penknife with a warning click and threw his leg into place.

"All I have to say is, if my dancing ever caused anybody to stumble, he couldn't stand up if I didn't."

"It were better for a millstone to be tied around your neck, and that you were sunk in the bottom of the sea," cried Daphne's father, gathering up his bridle-reins.

"Sink or swim, I'm going to dance," said Hilary. "But it's all nonsense. You are quoting texts to me that don't apply to my case. And you ought to know it. If you are going to turn me out of the church, it ought not to be for dancing. It ought to be for worse things — things that I am sorry for, but that I do. And there is one thing that I don't want you to misunderstand: all that I have said has been against *you*, remember, and not against the Bible; and to my mind there is a difference."

He rose from his plough as he spoke, and looked from the one to the other of them with his face growing solemn as he concluded: "Turn me out! But you will have to answer for the consequences. You know how this hurts a young man at the beginning of his life — at the beginning of his temptations and real struggles, when you old people ought to help him."

He stepped behind his plough and started his horse with a quiet, friendly cluck.

The next Sunday the elders and the deacons

rode gravely to church through the June woods, and sat as an ecclesiastical body on the front seat. The gravest among them was Daphne's father, who at intervals held to his nose a green walnut which he had pulled on the way, as was often his wont at this season. He smelled at it in long, devoted, audible draughts, as if fearing that otherwise he might be annoyed with the odour of brimstone. At the proper moment he arose and laid the case before the church with a recommendation, and the congregation thereupon withdrew its membership from Hilary. On the way home Daphne's father, who was in all things a walnut-smelling person of the most superior sort, forbade her to receive any further attentions from him.

The next day he met Hilary in the lane and drew in his nag, but without any greeting.

"Your bull has been breaking through my fences again," he said. "I want you to keep him at home hereafter."

"If you kept your fences up," the young farmer replied bluntly, "my bull wouldn't break through them. He never breaks through my fences." He was talking to another farmer now, not to an elder of the church, and his manner was fiercer.

"You've no right to keep any such dangerous animal in the neighbourhood," insisted the elder hotly.

"Right or wrong, I keep him," replied Hilary. "A bull that didn't have spirit enough in him to jump *some* fences wouldn't be of any use to me. But, of course, I know that troubles in the church keep you busy."

His clear eyes rested with sarcastic mischief on the elder, who rose suddenly in his stirrups, as though he would have struck him.

"Never do you darken my door again, sir," he said, his voice getting thick with anger, "or speak to a member of my family," and he drove his heels into his horse's ribs and started off.

The boy sat still for a moment looking after him.

"If he only were about my age," he said slowly to himself, "or anywhere under fifty."

And then he spurred forward and rode beside him.

"There was one question I wanted to ask you," he said savagely.

The elder glared at him without speaking.

"I've heard you say the church was meant to save sinners. I reckon you wouldn't object to my coming to church the same as before?"

And the next Sunday he was back in his old seat. A thrill shot through the congregation at the sight of this black sheep of the fold, whose very wool now seemed to smell ominously all over the church. So that Daphne's father produced his green walnut at once; and his prayer had that peculiar tone in which men sometimes virtually say to the Almighty that He can rely upon them to see that all sinners are duly punished.

Hilary could watch Daphne from where he sat; and during the prayer Daphne, under a pretext, opened her eyes to get her handkerchief and glanced at him. When their eyes met, his face took on a smile of victory and contempt. In return Daphne gave him a smile of the wickedest approval; and if they had ridden all day in his buggy, she could not better have expressed her forgiveness for his rudeness to her at the picnic and in the field.

VIII

Has it ever been remarked that when a scandal like this occurs in a country neighbourhood, somebody soon afterwards gives a dinner to several ladies? The connection of terrestrial happenings is not always clear. Who would suspect that a calm, remote, little thing like the moon could so trouble the seas? Or that the dark side of it brings the waters rushing together as tumultuously as the bright?

The Thursday following there was one of these dinners, and it was one of those long, dry, summer days when the ladies arrive with freshly starched faces before it gets hot, and leave with freshly starched faces after it gets cool.

The guests, although having that sense of bodily comfort which precedes the certainty of delicacies and which makes people kindly and confidential in advance, were sitting together in the forenoon amid the most frigid attempts to start a conversation. At last one of them ventured upon the dryest, simplest mention of Hilary's name. After that the deluge.

They reviewed his entire past. One told how, as a little boy, he had always come into church with the other members of the family, and sung out of a hymn-book with his mother; but in the last few years had waited outside with the fast young men of the neighbourhood, keeping a purely secular eye upon the girls in the carriages as they drove up to the steps. Another remembered that he regularly marched in at the head of these upon the singing of the last hymn, and sat far back among the hardened and the backsliders; and that sometimes he whittled matches, more than one of which exploded with a loud crack close to the ear of one of the most venerable sisters in the fold; that if the sermon was long, he snapped his watch at the preacher loud enough for half the congregation to hear; that at times he did not come to church at all, but was away, no one knew where. A third recalled how he would never miss a circus in the neighbouring towns, and would often guy the clown in a voice to be heard above the uproar of the ring; that once being bantered by the clown in return, he had shed his coat and tried to ride the mule — and did ride it until the mule lay down and rolled on him. It was not forgotten that he had always been fond of the negro minstrel shows, where he picked up songs and the best of his jokes — to be retold on Saturday afternoons at the blacksmith shop, where the young farmers assembled to pitch quoits and hear the news. One of them had heard from her husband that he could be seen about the court-house square on county court days in the neighbouring counties, smoking constantly, shaking hands right and left, and followed by other young fellows trying to smoke and shake hands like him — all with a colour in their faces that did not come from the sun. It seems, also, that he would be the last to start home from town toward nightfall, and when he did start, whirled out of the livery stable in a curve that made the buggy reel; passing everybody on the way home, over rocks, ruts, culverts, bridges, and those long piles of cracked limestone that are so terrible to a horse's feet. It was not related, however, that once in this way he had spun so dizzily around two old jogging neighbours of his — husbands of two of these ladies — that they had spoken up feelingly on the subject of old Bourbon, and the better to illustrate to each other the proper use of this wily spirit, had produced a confidential bottle from under the buggy-seat and exchanged their "regards." But it was known that once he had come in unsteadily upon one of these good old men as he warmed himself at the office stove of the livery stable, had sat down in his lap, and throwing his arms around him had challenged him to billiards for fried oysters.

By degrees the conversation drifted into darker channels as the caldron bubbled more furiously — being so richly fed. They recalled, with low, sad voices, the fact that about two years before this he had been sent as a student to the State college, and after a short career had returned home disgraced. And since then he had become wilder; the hurrying hoof-beats of his little mare could be heard up and down the turnpike long after midnight, miles away from home. What was the meaning of those songs of his, always of the same tenor?

From this point the talk, if submitted for print, must have lost in volume by reason of expurgations. The whole conversation might have made Dr. Johnson's ideal book: one consisting of a preface, setting forth what it would contain, followed by an appendix stating why it did not contain it.

Daphne and her mother were among the company. The girl had sat silent thus far, her head bent low over her needle-work.

Her mother, also, had taken little part in the talk. She was one of the crushed and silent women. The wives of such elders usually are. When she spent a day abroad, her habit of silence lay on her still. Her conversation consisted mainly of replies to questions. If she volunteered a remark, it was usually a quotation or a timid interpretation of her husband's opinions. She never dared quote or interpret him to his face; and this boldness behind his back was the last strain of vivacity in her that survived his desolating tyranny.

At last the conversation turned on the subject of the picnic, and then she felt emboldened to make a remark:

"My husband will never forgive him for taking advantage of a child like Daphne. He felt the disgrace of it terribly on account of his position in the church."

Daphne here dropped her sewing as though it were a coal.

"Now, mother, *you* hush," she exclaimed. Her lips were white and quivering with anger and with the heartache of those two infinite hours. And they had been sitting there without observing her! They saw her now, and such a silence filled the room that the sounds of insect life out in the yard were heard through the open doors and windows. Daphne picked up her work again and bent her head lower. But the silence lasted; and feeling that their eyes were turned on her like burning-glasses, and that it was too late now ever to undo the scandal of her words, she folded her hands and fixed her eyes on her mother again.

"You know that I am not a child," she said. "You know that Hilary did not take any advantage of me. You know that I did not disgrace anybody. And father knows it. Then why do you say so? I'll tell you why I danced, if you want to know. And I'll tell him when I get home. And why don't you keep out of this gossip? I am sick of it," she continued excitedly, her eyes flashing as she looked round upon them all. "And you are no better than mischief-makers. What you've been saying are *lies!*" She flirted out of the room with a backward toss of her head and taking her seat on the porch went on with her work.

This spoiled the dinner. One cannot perfectly enjoy the hospitality of a hostess whom one has just accused of telling lies, and the hostess does not perfectly enjoy having one try. But great things were possible to the company that day. Daphne at the table was so pressed with attentions from her hostess and the guests that the occasion was as good as an ovation in her honour. She was glad enough to smooth over the rupture; for she was secretly terrified by the thought that they would misunderstand her motive in taking Hilary's part, and make a neighbourhood scandal of that. Simple, seventeen-year-old Daphne! As if those wiseacres did not understand perfectly now what the matter was, and as if one-half of them were not already preparing to tell the other half that they had known it all the time.

The ladies separated into groups of twos and threes immediately after dinner and strolled away on their quiet little biological walks, some around the flower-beds in the front yard, some to look at the grapes and young vegetables in the garden; and then it was that they began to give each other nudges that were as long as paragraphs and glances that would have filled a page. Daphne's mother having framed awkward excuses a little later for starting home,— some salt-rising had to be made for supper,— they came together again; and once more there followed a frigid effort to begin general conversation. One of them at last inquired Daphne's age, and everything else followed. It was like turning up a long open tube filled with shot. They did not even omit the story of how Daphne had as a child never cared for dolls, but liked better to play with little boys and was often caught hugging them. Another of the guests soon made excuses for leaving; and she availed herself of the extra time to drive by and talk the rest of the afternoon with Hilary's mother. And then, having made all the mischief she could in one day, at the close of it she felt so proud of herself, and so pleased with her virtues, that on the way home she leaned back in the corner of the rockaway, closed her eyes, folded her hands over her waist, and, unmindful even of the fact that she was crushing her bonnet, she sang over and over again her favourite hymn:

"Just as I am, without one plea!"

Pleasant to human nature are its lies!

Cutting words passed between Daphne and her father that night — words that life is too short to make forgotten. She was sitting at the window of her room as late as twelve o'clock, her eyes swollen and sobs still trembling on her lips. Poor child, poor Daphne! Any rebellion against the general order of things in this world was beyond her intelligence. Her quarrel with life directed itself against a dozen or more people as the wilful originators of all her grief and restlessness and pain; and she believed that as soon as she were rid of these, she would be perfectly happy. She had all the desires she wanted, and she would gratify these just as she chose.

She did not care enough for her father to have been deeply wounded by anything he said. But aroused to the idea that he was mainly responsible for her unhappiness, she recalled the things she had against him as far back in life as she could remember.

There is no earthly tribunal so terrible, both in its justice and in its injustice, as the mind of a child bent upon finding out why it turns against a parent. It always does find out; and Daphne's memory fished up some black and curious things from the river of the past.

She was too young to make allowances for his faults, and perhaps she was too truly his child to have been able to show him the mercy that he denied to her. The young never realize when judging the old that the old are in a measure irresponsible and guiltless. The old themselves never fully understand why it is that despite all their wisdom and struggles they do not become better than they are. Daphne could not see generations of faulty people darkening away behind her father and handing down to him their injustice, hardness, unlovableness, their warped and purblind consciences; could not see that he could no more help being what he was than she could help being what she was: so that both of them might well have been more patient and forgiving with each other. But it takes a great deal of inner light to see this outer darkness enveloping our life, and a great deal of goodness to walk sweetly forward through it.

Of one fact during these unhappy hours she remained unaware: that whenever she was thinking of her father her tears ceased; and whenever she was remembering Hilary they flowed again. Those stories about his life in the town while he was a student and of his expulsion from college—were they true? Those midnight rides and songs ever since—did they mean what those old mothers had said they meant?

Among all the terrible things her father had said, the chief one with which he had frightened her, was the idea that she had now made herself the subject of a new and more serious neighbourhood scandal. And most of all, he had forbidden her ever to see Hilary again.

Nevertheless the plan which Daphne had been forming all night was to see Hilary once more as soon as possible. Scandal or no scandal, she must let him know that she had taken his part as his friend, and correct any false impression that he might have formed of her character and her motive.

Then she would tell him that it was the last time they could meet, and say good-by. And then—she would always live a sad and lonely woman in this dark and dreary world. Daphne was so soothed and cheered by the future image of herself as a sad and lonely woman in a dark and dreary world, that she got into bed immediately and had a delicious sleep.

Through her sleep she was out in the green meadow, and he was coming down the path to meet her. Once in the vividness of the vision she stretched out her arms: her lips parted and her bosom heaved with a long, deep breath of peace.

Love had at least taken possession of her dreams: and Love knows that dreams are often the most important thing to capture.

IX

Hilary's mother was waiting for him when he reached home late that night. For years they had spread the report, as they always do, that he had broken her heart. If so, she idolized him with the fragments. Not a night in all that time but she placed a lamp in the window to guide him home across the storm-swept fields; in winter kept the fire bright for him; made him draw off his soaking or frozen boots for a warm foot-bath; wiped his feet in her own lap, pressing them jealously against her heart; asked no questions; thought no wrong; watched with devoted eyes his face with the flickering firelight on it, now thoughtful, now happy with the pleasure of things in which he allowed her no share; when he was in bed, often stole into his room to give a last tuck to his feet and touch his forehead with her lips; and afterwards prayed for him in tears and with pride at her own shining pillow; a divine love and trust, which is perhaps the best anchor that we men can ever be held by during those raging years.

The front door stood open, a swinging lamp burned low in the hall, and as he walked up the pavement, having taken the bridle and saddle off his mare, he saw the soft, slow movement of her fan. He sat down at her feet, leaning against a white Corinthian column, and took out a cigar.

"Don't smoke yet," she said, and she brought him a saucer of his favourite cream and a plate of his favourite cake. He was in one of his quiet moods, and ate it in silence. But she knew how to wait. Then he lighted his cigar.

"You'd better go to bed, mother," he said gently. He liked to talk of her as though she were a child.

"It's too hot. Surely it will rain to-morrow. It has been lightning in the north." She leaned forward and looked intently at the sky as if a shower were the only thing in the world she could be minding.

"The corn needs it."

"And the garden — everything."

"Has anybody been here to see me since dinner?"

"No. Somebody has been to see *me*."

"One of your beaux?"

"Never you mind."

She often coquetted with him. Southern women characteristically do with their grown sons. It is the lingering remnant of an old prodigal habit.

"I *know!* I saw her rockaway."

"I don't believe it. Who was she?"

"Never *you* mind. And I can guess what she came for."

"What?"

"To tell you about the dinner to-day."

She did not reply at once. When she did, her words had the calm of a coming storm.

"She *did* tell me about that."

He remained silent, not being further interested; and her fan moved before her face with slow precision.

"Hilary!"

"Yes'm."

"There was a disgraceful scene at that dinner to-day."

"There always is at that house, isn't there? Isn't that the reason you and the others who were invited didn't go?"

"I don't mean that now!"

Her tone caught his ear as unusual. Moreover, when his mother said that anything was disgraceful, it was disgraceful.

She began and told him, — not exactly the facts, — but what had been reported as facts; and naturally her informant had not repeated what the ladies had said about her own son. It is remarkable that a woman who is not a gossip will believe a gossip when the tale flows in with the current of her anxieties. Hilary's mother had in mind the girl that she wanted him to marry. The recent coupling of his name with Daphne's aroused her to prompt decisive action.

He listened without comment; but his cigar went out; he was interested.

The old clock behind the door in the hall struck one. She rose and stood over him.

"It is not a delicate thing for a mother to say to a son, and you know that I have never said such a thing to you. But"— her tone was gentle, merciless — "the girl is in love with you, and she has shown it, and it will be talked about all over the neighbourhood. Keep away from her! She is not the kind of a girl you want to have anything to do with. There are some things I can't very well explain to you, but if I must I will!"

One of her hands sought for his forehead under his heavy hair.

"Good-night," she murmured, and she bent down and laid her lips on it.

He threw away his cigar, and putting up his arms drew her face down to his like a child.

When she reached the doorway of the hall, she turned.

"Would you like to know now what I mean?" Her voice was calm and determined.

"No'm. Good-night."

His setter got up from where it had been lying on the other side of the porch, and stretched itself beside him. He lighted a cigar.

Young men of twenty do not care much for what their mothers may think about girls. The world has grown a deal wiser since mothers understood that subject, if they ever did. These sons, on the other hand, have mastered that branch of knowledge. Hilary considered himself a man who was able to do his own thinking; and it afforded him now some amusement that his mother should undertake, at this late day, to give him advice about his own specialty.

But he began to turn over the account he had received of the day's doings. It struck him that the girl, arraigned before that tribunal of women, was a good deal like himself, when summoned of old before the faculty of the college. She had honestly told them what she thought of them, and he on one occasion had told the faculty in pretty much the same terms what he thought of them. He liked her spirit immensely, and he resolved, the first chance he could get, to let her know it.

And then she had declined to allow the blame of the dancing to rest on him — that fact had been incidentally dropped by his mother as it had been incidentally imparted by the tale-bearer. His heart warmed to her for this. He remembered how he had once fought a student for involving him without ground in a college scrape, when he had scrapes enough of his own. It was fair-minded in her; and fair play was a thing that he might have prided himself upon having always tried to practise. It was courageous in her; and he did not respect anybody — man or woman — who was not courageous.

Altogether he liked better the way she had acted in the whole matter than his own conduct; for he had certainly helped to get her into the trouble, and it had not even occurred to him to try to help her out. Now she was more deeply in than ever. She had bearded those old gossips in their den. They would never forgive her, and they would have their revenge. That was why they had already started this new scandal that she was in love with him. And when they had used that scandal against her until they got tired of it, they would invent some other. He was in a position to know what this kind of rapid ineradicable scandal-growth meant. Experience had taught him. In his own case he had gone on in his own way, and had left everything to settle itself, or to unsettle itself, as it chose or did not choose; and he would no more have taken the trouble to turn upon his vilifiers than he would have made a trip to the woods for the purpose of stamping out the toadstools; some would be dying by the time he got there, and others would be springing up the moment he was gone.

But his mother's last words about Daphne — what did they mean? What were those things about her that she could not explain to him? If he had been a gentleman, of course, he would have let that question go unanswered. But he was not quite a gentleman, and he resolved to see her and find out for himself. As for asking his mother to tell him, or even allowing her to tell him — he tossed his cigar out into the grass.

And as for letting any amount of gossip that had influenced or might hereafter influence his mother prejudice him against the girl who had befriended him — his state of mind on that subject was also expressed by the same gesture.

They were close to Nature as they lay there that summer night — those two young animals. The dog was the better trained, and had behind him generations of better trained fathers; for what is it to train a whole race of dogs in comparison with a single human being — the very breath of whose life is error?

The dog at best would have made but a poor sort of human creature; but the fellow would at least have made a noble dog. He had the sovereign qualities of courage and faithfulness and affection, with no mean order of sagacity; and if he hunted much, at least he always hunted fairly and in the open field.

Take a cannon-ball of the best metal that may be cast. Hollow it out. Fill it with water. Plug it tight. Put it under the corner of a house, so that the weight of the house will rest on the plug. Then let Nature come along in a freezing mood, and one of two things will happen: the water will force the plug and lift the house, or the ball will burst. And if she requires so much room in which to freeze, think of the space that she needs for heat! Nature quietly asks room for the operations of her laws; if it is not given, she takes it, and you take the consequences. If the young man's life had overflowed the innocent banks of childhood, if wild oats seem to spring up wherever he had trod, you could not have gotten from him any intelligent account of what he was doing. You would have had to question Nature and his forefathers, and some of the people who had always influenced him.

He had never had a moral friend among his young neighbourhood associates; if he had had one, he would not have believed in him; and for many a generation, perhaps, he had not had a strictly moral male ancestor. What chance was there for him, even before he was born, ever to see and to love the right as it is seen and loved by the right-minded? What chance was there for him, after birth, to grow up unlike those who taught him their ways of life before he was old enough to understand there are other and better ways — the only true ones? When he was a little fellow also, going around with his father, he often fell into the company of a group of old farmers who were cracking broad jokes at each other with great laughter, or telling stories about their young days. He looked up to these big, burly, ruddy men; he felt ashamed that he alone of the company had no good stories to tell about himself, and he determined to have the stories by and by.

By and by he had them. They will not be told here — except one which has been darkly hinted at. It is scant credit to him — but it is justice, nevertheless — to have it known in its truth.

One autumn he had been sent as a student

to the State college, and a room engaged for him in the dormitories, in order that he might fall more closely under the fatherly care of the president. Up to the following Christmas he fell at intervals under the fatherly care of the entire faculty.

His career as an academician ranged through the tenets of many unlike systems of philosophy, and by turns he was everything except one thing only — he was never platonic.

In a few weeks after his entering, the top of his bureau and the edge of his looking-glass blossomed out into a bower of the photographs of the girls he soon met, and of actresses whom he had never seen but whose curves and poses struck his fancy. He soon wore the bloom off of two cadet uniforms; and on Saturday afternoons was much in evidence walking along Main street in the tarnished splendour of one of these — a cigarette in his fingers, his heavy front of yellow hair hanging forward as a bang under the lip of his gray cap, and his glance roving about for anything feminine and attractive that passed and would notice him. He spent a good deal of time around the livery stables, where he took part with the men in the talk about stock and crops, and occasionally met farmers from his neighbourhood. In his college society, they quickly chose him as a marshal at their open sessions; and on these occasions, gorgeous in sash, rosette, and white gloves, he would guide the company to their seats — ushering the girls along with an official pressure of their beautiful soft arms, the real nature of which did not deceive them, however. And now and then he made a recitation that fairly took the breath of a professor away, merely to show everybody that he was not a fool.

The downfall of his scholastic career came about through a cornet. Being of a musical turn, he had entered the college band, and had elected to play upon that instrument, which is known to be of a most uncertain performance in the wind when not kept strictly to its better and more reasonable nature. His favourite hours of practice he thought would be in his room at night; but he was soon admonished that this was not allowable. Occasionally, however, he would allow himself one vagrant blast — he called it blowing the dust out of Gabriel's throat — that awoke the sleepers around, leaving them to regain their dreams as best they could.

One night he had come from the theatre — after an hour or more about town — and he was feeling ungovernably alive; and when he got into his room and lighted his student's lamp, and did not wish to go to bed, and did not wish to get his lessons, the spirit of the cornet came upon him, and swearing that he would practise when and where he pleased, he reached for — Gabriel.

Across the hall opposite Hilary's room was the room of a tall, green sapling from the foothills of the Cumberland — a transplanted sapling that had swayed backward and forward till midnight before an awful thing called Greek, and that meant to get up at five o'clock the next morning and sway on, as it had been swaying for the three months past. Meantime the sapling asked for rest.

Hilary had hardly begun to woo the ear of night with his fingering fantasies, when his door was flung open, and the sapling stood in the doorway, his short shirt fluttering about his thin loins, and his legs rising from the floor to his slab trunk like a pair of long, yellow ivory compasses.

The musician was sitting in his chair with his face toward the door, his eyes blinking softly like a cat's before a fire, and his cheeks puffed out like an old picture of Boreas.

The storm-swept sapling said something — that was drowned by the music — and waited. Then he spoke again and waited. Then he advanced his compasses and with one leg of them, and an inconceivable nimbleness for anything so rigid, kicked Gabriel against the ceiling with a crash; and then — there was called a meeting of the faculty the next afternoon, and the young Kentucky highlander and the young Kentucky lowlander attended the meeting.

The complaints of a faculty are often like the janitor's keys — a bunch gradually made up of little and large, so that whenever they care to use one they can have them all. Hilary was invited to examine a surprising bunch of keys, and to testify to what kind of a door each key unlocked. He quietly acknowledged to the big keys, but of the little ones grew heady and contemptuous, going so far as to say that the faculty made as much trouble about nothing as a lot of old cats at night on a backyard fence. What right had they to pry into a young fellow's outside affairs? Suppose the students were to pry into *their* outside affairs? What was sauce for the gander ought to be good sauce for the gosling, etc., etc.

The first light snows of the year were falling. The Thanksgiving gobbler had been selected at home. The quails were fat in the fields, and the rabbits were nibbling the cabbages in the gardens. His setter missed him sadly. He and the faculty held irreconcilable views of life and discipline; and once more the sapling swayed on undisturbed before the tongue of Pericles.

X

The sunlight grew pale the following morning; a shadow crept rapidly over the blue; bolts darted about the skies like maddened redbirds; the thunder, ploughing its way down the dome as along zigzag cracks in a stony street, filled the caverns of the horizon with reverberations that shook the earth; and the rain was whirled across the landscape in long, white, wavering sheets. Then all day quiet and silence throughout Nature except for the drops, tapping high and low the twinkling leaves; except for the new melody of woodland and meadow brooks, late silvery and with a voice only for their pebbles and moss and mint, but now yellow and brawling and leaping back into the grassy channels that were their old-time beds; except for the indoor music of dripping caves and rushing gutters and overflowing rain-barrels. And when at last in the gold of the cool west the sun broke from the edge of the gray, over what a green, soaked, fragrant world he reared the arch of Nature's peace!

Not a little blade of corn in the fields but holds in an emerald vase its treasure of white gems. The hemp-stalks bend so low under the weight of their plumes, that were a vesper sparrow to alight on one for his evening hymn, it would go with him to the ground. The leaning barley and rye and wheat flash in the last rays their jewelled beards. Under the old apple-trees, golden-brown mushrooms are already pushing upward through the leaf-loam, rank with many an autumn's dropping. About the yards the peonies fall with faces earthward. In the stable-lots the larded porkers, with bristles as clean as frost, and flesh of pinky whiteness, are hunting with nervous nostrils for the lush purslane. The fowls are driving their bills up and down their wet breasts. And the farmers who have been shelling corn for the mill come out of their barns, with their coats over their shoulders, on the way to supper, look about for the plough-horses, and glance at the western sky, from which the last drops are falling.

But soon only a more passionate heat shoots from the sun into the planet. The plumes of the hemp are so dry again, that by the pollen shaken from their tops you can trace the young rabbits making their way out to the dusty paths. The shadows of white clouds sail over purple stretches of bluegrass, hiding the sun from the steady eye of the turkey, whose brood is spread out before her like a fan on the earth. At early morning the neighing of the stallions is heard around the horizon; at noon the bull makes the deep, hot pastures echo with his majestic summons; out in the blazing meadows the butterflies strike the afternoon air with more impatient wings; under the moon all night the play of ducks and drakes goes on along the margins of the ponds. Young people are running away and marrying; middle-aged farmers surprise their wives by looking in on them at their butter-making in the sweet dairies; and Nature is lashing everything — grass, fruit, insects, cattle, human creatures —

more fiercely onward to the fulfilment of her ends. She is the great heartless haymaker, wasting not a ray of sunshine on a clod, but caring naught for the light that beats upon a throne, and holding man and woman, with their longing for immortality, and their capacities for joy and pain, as of no more account than a couple of fertilizing nasturtiums.

The storm kept Daphne at home. On the next day the earth was yellow with sunlight, but there were puddles along the path, and a branch rushing swollen across the green valley in the fields. On the third, her mother took the children to town to be fitted with hats and shoes, and Daphne also, to be freshened up with various moderate adornments, in view of a protracted meeting soon to begin. On the fourth, some ladies dropped in to spend the day, bearing in mind the episode at the dinner, and having grown curious to watch events accordingly. On the fifth, her father carried out the idea of cutting down some cedar-trees in the front yard for fence posts; and whenever he was working about the house, he kept her near to wait on him in unnecessary ways. On the sixth, he rode away with two hands and an empty wagon-bed for some work on the farm; her mother drove off to another dinner — dinners never cease in Kentucky, and the wife of an elder is not free to decline invitations; and at last she was left alone in the front porch, her face turned with burning eagerness toward the fields. In a little while she had slipped away.

All these days Hilary had been eager to see her. He was carrying a good many girls in his mind that summer; none in his heart; but his plans concerning these latter were for the time forgotten. He hung about that part of his farm from which he could have descried her in the distance. Each forenoon and afternoon, at the usual hour of her going to her uncle's, he rode over and watched for her. Other people passed to and fro, — children and servants, — but not Daphne; and repeated disappointments fanned his desire to see her.

When she came into sight at last, he was soon walking beside her, leading his horse by the reins.

"I have been waiting to see you, Daphne," he said, with a smile, but general air of seriousness. "I have been waiting a long time for a chance to talk to you."

"And I have wanted to see you," said Daphne, her face turned away and her voice hardly to be heard. "I have been waiting for a chance to talk to you."

The change in her was so great, so unexpected, it contained an appeal to him so touching, that he glanced quickly at her. Then he stopped short and looked searchingly around the meadow.

The thorn-tree is often the only one that can survive on these pasture lands. Its spikes, even when it is no higher than the grass, keep off the mouths of grazing stock. As it grows higher, birds see it standing solitary in the distance and fly to it, as a resting-place in passing. Some autumn day a seed of the wild grape is thus dropped near its root; and in time the thorn-tree and the grape-vine come to thrive together.

As Hilary now looked for some shade to

which they could retreat from the blinding, burning sunlight, he saw one of these standing off at a distance of a few hundred yards. He slipped the bridle-reins through the headstall, and giving his mare a soft slap on the shoulder, turned her loose to graze.

"Come over here and sit down out of the sun," he said, starting off in his authoritative way. "I want to talk to you."

Daphne followed in his wake through the deep grass.

When they reached the tree, they sat down under the rayless boughs. Some sheep lying there ran round to the other side and stood watching them, with a frightened look in their clear, peaceful eyes.

"What's the matter?" he said, fanning his face, and tugging with his forefinger to loosen his shirt-collar from his moist neck. He had the manner of a powerful comrade who means to succour a weaker one.

"Nothing," said Daphne like a true woman.

"Yes, but there is," he insisted. "I got you into trouble. I didn't think of that when I asked you to dance."

"You had nothing to do with it," retorted Daphne, with a flash. "I danced for spite."

He threw back his head with a peal of laughter. All at once this was broken off. He sat up, with his eyes fixed on the lower edge of the meadow.

"Here comes your father," he said gravely.

Daphne turned. Her father was riding slowly through the bars. A wagon-bed loaded with rails crept slowly after him.

In an instant the things that had cost her so much toil and so many tears to arrange, — her explanations, her justifications, and her parting, — all the reserve and the coldness that she had laid up in her heart, as one fills high a little ice-house with fear of far-off summer heat — all were quite gone, melted away. And everything that he had planned to tell her was forgotten also at the sight of that stern figure on horseback bearing unconsciously down upon them.

"If I had only kept my mouth shut about his old fences," he said to himself. "Confound my bull!" and he looked anxiously at Daphne, who sat with her eyes riveted on her father. The next moment she had turned, and they were laughing in each other's faces.

"What shall I do?" she cried, leaning over and burying her face in her hands, and lifting it again scarlet with excitement.

"Don't do anything," he said calmly.

"But, Hilary, if he sees us we are lost."

"If he sees us, we are found."

"But he mustn't see me here!" she cried, with something like real terror. "I believe I'll lie down in the grass. Maybe he'll think I'm a friend of yours."

"My friends all sit up in the grass," said Hilary.

But Daphne had already hidden.

Many a time when a little girl she had amused herself by screaming like a hawk at the young guineas, and seeing them cuddle invisible under small tufts and weeds. Out in the stable-lot where the grass was grazed so close that the geese could barely nip it, she would sometimes get one of the negro men to scare the little pigs, for the delight of seeing them squat as though hidden, when they were no more hidden than if they had spread themselves out upon so many dinner dishes. All of us reveal traces of this primitive instinct upon occasion. Daphne was doing her best to hide now.

When Hilary realized it he moved in front of her, screening her as well as possible.

"Hadn't you better lie down, too?" she asked.

"No," he replied quickly.

"But if he sees you, he might take a notion to ride over this way!"

"Then he'll have to ride."

"But, Hilary, suppose he were to find me lying down here behind you, hiding?"

"Then he'll have to find you."

"You get me into trouble and then you won't help me out!" exclaimed Daphne with considerable heat.

"It might not make matters any better for me to hide," he answered quietly. "But if he comes over here and tries to get us into trouble, I'll see then what I can do."

Daphne lay silent for a moment, thinking.

Then she nestled more closely down, and said with gay unconscious archness:

"I'm not hiding because I'm afraid of him. I'm doing it just because I want to." She did not know that the fresh happiness flushing her at that moment came from the fact of having Hilary between herself and her father as a protector; that she was drinking in the delight a woman feels in getting playfully behind the man she loves in the face of danger; but her action bound her to him and brought her more under his influence.

His words showed that he also felt his position — the position of the male who stalks forth from the herd and stands the silent challenger. He was young, and vain of his manhood in the usual innocent way that led him to carry the chip on his shoulder for the world to knock off; and he placed himself before Daphne with the understanding that if they were discovered, there would be trouble. Her father was a violent man, and the circumstances were not such that any Kentucky father would overlook them. But with his inward seriousness, his face wore its usual look of reckless unconcern.

"Is he coming this way?" asked Daphne, after an interval of impatient waiting.

"Straight ahead. Are you hid?"

"I can't see whether I'm hid or not. Where is he now?"

"Right on us."

"Does he see you?"

"Yes."

"Do you think he sees me?"

"I'm sure of it."

"Then I might as well get up," said Daphne with the courage of despair, and up she got. Her father was riding along the path in front of them, but not looking. She was down again like a partridge.

"How could you fool me, Hilary? Suppose he *had* been looking!"

"I wonder what he thinks I'm doing, sitting over here in the grass like a stump," said Hilary. "If he takes me for one, he must think I've got an awful lot of roots."

"Tell me when it's time to get up."

"I will."

He turned softly toward her. She was lying on her side, with her burning cheek in one hand. The other hand rested high on the curve of her hip. Her braids had fallen forward, and lay in a heavy loop about her lovely shoulders. Her eyes were closed, her scarlet lips parted in a smile. The edges of her snow-white petticoats showed beneath her blue dress, and beyond these one of her feet and ankles. Nothing more fragrant with innocence ever lay on the grass.

"Is it time to get up now?"

"Not yet," and he sat bending over her.

"Now?"

"Not yet," he repeated more softly.

"Now, then?"

"Not for a long time."

His voice thrilled her, and she glanced up at him. His laughing eyes were glowing down upon her under his heavy mat of hair. She sat up and looked toward the wagon crawling away in the distance: her father was no longer in sight.

One of the ewes, dissatisfied with a back view, stamped her forefoot impatiently, and ran round in front, and out into the sun. Her lambs followed; and the three, ranging themselves abreast, stared at Daphne with a look of helpless inquiry.

"Sh-pp-pp!" she cried, throwing up her hands at them, irritated. "Go away!"

They turned and ran; the others followed; and the whole number, falling into line, took a path meekly homeward. They left a greater sense of privacy under the tree. Several yards off was a small stock pond. Around the edge of this the water stood hot and green in the tracks of the cattle and the sheep, and about these pools the yellow butterflies were thick, alighting daintily on the promontories of the mud, or rising two by two through the dazzling atmosphere in columns of enamoured flight.

Daphne leaned over to the bluegrass where it swayed unbroken in the breeze, and drew out of their sockets several stalks of it, bearing on their tops the purplish seed-vessels. With them she began to braid a ring about one of her fingers in the old simple fashion of the country.

As they talked, he lay propped on his elbow, watching her fingers, the soft slow movements of which little by little wove a spell over his eyes. And once again the power of her beauty began to draw him beyond control. He felt a desire to seize her hands, to crush them in his. His eyes passed upward along her tapering wrists, the skin of which was like mother-of-pearl; upward along the arm to the shoulder — to her neck — to her deeply crimsoned cheeks — to the purity of her brow — to the purity of her eyes, the downcast lashes of which hid them like conscious fringes.

An awkward silence began to fall between them. Daphne felt that the time had come for her to speak. But powerless to begin, she feigned to busy herself all the more devotedly with braiding the deep green circlet. Suddenly he drew himself through the grass to her side.

"Let *me!*"

"No!" she cried, lifting her arm above

his reach and looking at him with a gay threat. "You don't know how."

"I do know how," he said with his white teeth on his red under-lip, and his eyes sparkling; and reaching upward, he laid his hand in the hollow of her elbow and pulled her arm down.

"No! No!" she cried again, putting her hands behind her back. "You will spoil it!"

"I will not spoil it," he said, moving so close to her that his breath was on her face, and reaching around to unclasp her hands.

"No! No! No!" she cried, bending away from him. "I don't want any ring!" and she tore it from her finger and threw it out on the grass. Then she got up, and brushing the grass seed off her lap put on her hat.

He sat cross-legged on the grass before her. He had put on his hat and the brim hid his eyes.

"And you are not going to stay and talk to me?" he said in a tone of reproachfulness without looking up.

She was excited and weak and trembling,

and so she put out her hand and took hold of a strong loop of the grape-vine hanging from a branch of the thorn, and laid her cheek against her hand and looked away from him.

"I thought you were better than the others," he continued with the bitter wisdom of twenty years. "But you women are all alike. When a man gets into trouble, you desert him. You hurry him on to the devil. I have been turned out of the church, and now you are down on me. Oh, well! But you know how much I have always liked you, Daphne."

It was not the first time that he had acted this character. It had been a favourite rôle. But Daphne had never seen the like. She was overwhelmed with happiness that he cared so much for her; and to have him reproach her for indifference, and see him suffering with the idea that she had turned against him — that instantly changed the whole situation. He had not heard then what had taken place at the dinner. Under the circumstances, feeling certain that the secret of her love had not been discovered, she grew emboldened to risk a little more.

So she turned toward him smiling, and swayed gently as she clung to the vine.

"Yes; I have my orders not even to speak to you! Never again!" she said with the air of tantalizing.

"Then stay with me awhile now," he said, and lifted slowly to her his appealing face. She sat down, and screened herself with a little feminine transparency.

"I can't stay long: it's going to rain!"

He cast a wicked glance at the sky from under his hat: there were a few clouds on the horizon.

"And so you are never going to speak to me again," he said mournfully.

"Never!" How delicious her laughter was.

"I'll put a ring on your finger to remember me by."

He lay over in the grass and pulled several stalks. Then he lifted his eyes beseechingly to hers.

"Will you let me?"

Daphne hid her hands. He drew himself to her side and took one of them forcibly from her lap.

With a slow caressing movement he began to braid the grass ring around her finger — in and out, around and around, his fingers laced with her fingers, his palm lying close upon her palm, his blood tingling through the skin upon her blood. He made the braiding go wrong and took it off and began over again. Two or three times she drew a deep breath, and stole a bewildered look at his face, which was so close to hers that his hair brushed it — so close that she heard the quiver of his own breath. Then all at once he folded his hands about hers with a quick, fierce tenderness and looked up at her. She turned her face aside and tried to draw her hand away. His clasp tightened. She snatched it away and got up with a nervous laugh.

"Look at the butterflies! Aren't they pretty?"

He sprang up and tried to seize her hand again.

"You shan't go home yet!" he said in an undertone.

"Shan't I?" she said, backing away from him. "Who's going to keep me?"

"*I am*," he said, laughing excitedly and following her closely.

"My father's coming!" she cried out as a warning.

He turned and looked: there was no one in sight.

"He *is* coming — sooner or later!" she called.

She had retreated several yards off into the sunlight of the meadow.

The remembrance of the risk that he was causing her to run checked him. He went over to her.

"When can I see you again — soon?"

He had never spoken so seriously to her before. He had never before been so serious. But within the last hour Nature had been doing her work, and its effect was immediate. His sincerity instantly conquered her. Her eyes fell.

"No one has any right to keep us from seeing each other!" he insisted. "We must settle that for ourselves."

Daphne made no reply.

"But we can't meet here any more — with people passing backwards and forwards!" he continued rapidly and decisively. "What has happened to-day mustn't happen again."

"No!" she replied in a voice barely to be heard. "It must never happen again. We can't meet here."

They were walking side by side now toward the meadow path. As they reached it he paused:

"Come to the back of the pasture — to-morrow! — at four o'clock!" he said tentatively, recklessly.

Daphne did not answer as she moved away from him along the path homeward.

"Will you come?" he called out to her.

She turned and shook her head. Whatever her own new plans may have become, she was once more happy and laughing.

"Come, Daphne!"

She walked several paces further and turned and shook her head again.

"Come!" he pleaded.

She laughed at him.

He wheeled round to his mare grazing near. As he put his foot into the stirrup, he looked again: she was standing in the same place, laughing still.

"*You* go," she cried, waving him good-by. "There'll not be a soul to disturb you! To-morrow — at four o'clock!"

"Will you be there?" he said.

"Will you?" she answered.

"I'll be there to-morrow!" he said, "and every other day till you come."

XI

AN old ash-tree with a double trunk stood on the rear edge of the strip of woods where Daphne's father put his steers for summer pasture. Other forest trees grew near by; and past them ran the fence, low and rotting, which marked the troublesome boundary line between her father's and Hilary's farms. Blackberry bushes throve rank in some of the fence corners; in others poke-root towered amid low forests of the may-apple. Pawpaw-trees made a thicket on one side; and out in the pasture the ironweed, not cut until August, spread its purple fringes far above the grass.

No foot-path led that way. Chipmunks chased each other along the rails, gray and green in lichens, without a shriek, and scamper at the discovery of a looker-on. The sound of reapers in the nearest fields had a muffled faintness.

Toward this spot about five o'clock the following afternoon Daphne with simple trust was taking her way. From the moment when Hilary had opened up the possibility of her meeting him in secret, from the moment of believing that he was fond of her, life had become a new thing to Daphne and the world a better place. A home and past like hers had made little appeal to the better traits in her character; but neither had it yet destroyed them; and at once love began to soften and irradiate and ennoble her as it softens and irradiates and ennobles every soul who is able and worthy to feel it. She was kinder to them at home that day. When her father came in before dinner, hot and thirsty, she had ready for him a pitcher of lemonade — the drops standing like a heavy dew on the old Bohemian glass and a fragrance exhaling from the thin half-moons of lemon; and she brought it out on the porch to him as a surprise and with a novel playfulness. He drank the lemonade but did not thank her or notice her. His repulse caused her to turn with a fresh feeling of justification to this secret intercourse with Hilary.

As she entered the woods through a meadow, a butterfly, stirred from the weeds by her threatening feet, whirled itself upward into the wide, hot air and entered the woods also. Nature at that moment made no great difference between the insect and the girl in her instructions. She said to the butterfly: "Enter this woods. You may find what you seek — rest, honey, companionship." And she said to Daphne: "Enter this woods. You may find what you seek — rest from your restlessness, happiness, companionship." If the butterfly could have been asked why it cared for honey and for another butterfly of the opposite sex more than for anything else in the world, or why it was under the necessity of doing as Nature prompted it, there could have been no reply: and no more could a reply have been given to a like question by the child. But if the butterfly could have reasoned concerning the butterfly lot, its philosophy would perhaps have fallen into this strain:

"Truly among created things on this planet my life is the most unhappy. I alight with famishing zest upon one flower; others have been there before. I discover a fresh, splendid blossom that no one has touched: it is set so far inward among stems and thorns as to be out of my reach. I begin to drink at the brimming heart of a third, and lo! it is an old raindrop, bitter with rotting leaves. Entire days pass of heavenly brightness when I fly and fly and fly over fields without a blossom; then follow cold, wet ones, when I must lie hidden and wait. The least wind all but tears my wings from my body. I am made for perpetual calm, yet inhabit an earth of unending storms. Even to live, I must travel; no sooner have I moved my wings than I attract the attention of my enemies. There is no end of my perils and woes; and altogether, I am of all winged creatures least adapted to live on this globe. The upshot of the whole truth is that Nature allots me some moments of happiness during my one uncertain summer and impels me to make the most of these. So I do. I never decline honey when I want it and can get it."

Daphne would have given quite as simple account of why she was now going to meet Hilary in the woods. Not to have gone would have been like wasting one of the few chances of happiness in her unhappy life — like declining a new kind of delicious wild honey which Nature bade her seek as the chief thing in all the world.

She did not dream that she might be crossing the invisible boundary between moral light and darkness, or that she was advancing gaily toward those wastes of life over which women wander lost and die damned. If she could have known of the countless company of her sisters who have taken their first step toward the central tragedy of the world by doing what she now did — going to the first secret meeting with the men they have loved — if there could have flitted before her the vast pageant of the painted butterflies of her race, painted and torn and weary, and drooping all at last into the same foul mire — she might well have recoiled and tottered homeward an old woman, wrinkled with horror, her dark braids turned to snow.

But it was with Daphne this day as it has been with so many of the others. She had not yet learned what no woman who feels it can ever afterwards forget — the fear of herself. She had learned still less that a woman will risk herself with a man as though he had not himself to conquer or not to conquer. She lent her ear wholly to Nature who sat within her and played upon the ancient beguiling pipes of youth and innocence and trust and love. Many a girl has arisen from her seat wherever she has been in the world and gone out to answer these summonses as though they were divine. As for those great, solemn voices of warning that sound out in many other women at such moments — those despairing revengeful voices that perhaps sound in all women when it is too late — they were silent in this child. Even the bell of the divine casting that hangs in the mortal belfry of the soul tolled no alarm; the bell hung there, but motionless.

She was very lovely as she passed through the sunlight and shadow of the trees — lovelier than any psyche of the sun floating with moons of velvet jet on wings of heaven's blue — loveliest with the look of love thrilling in her; and no wild, lithe, gray leaper from tree-top to tree-top was ever more palpitant with animal life.

As she drew near the group of forest trees, she kept herself screened behind the ironweed and pawpaw-bushes. Some one else might be there. Would he be there? About ten yards off she paused and peeped through the thick boughs.

He was sitting at the root of the ash-tree with his face turned toward the opening through which he expected her to come. On the grass beside him lay his riding-gloves. On his knees, which were drawn up before him, he held a memorandum book, and in this he was scribbling. Now and then he would raise his eyes and watch for her, and frown with disappointment, and return to his lead-pencil.

Her eyes dwelt on him eagerly; her heart

beat loudly in her ears; an unwonted shyness urged her to slip away unseen.

A rabbit sat in its bed in the deep grass a few feet from where she stood, and growing suspicious of her, that she did not move on, leaped softly forth and ran across the open space past the tree to the fence behind. As it bounded by Hilary he threw his gloves at it from old boyish habit, and then, with a loud laugh, went and raked them out from under the briers. When he returned to the tree again, she was sitting quietly in his place.

"I thought you were never coming," she cried, mocking him reproachfully.

He stood staring at her in ludicrous surprise and delight.

"How did *you* get here?" he exclaimed. "Ride on that rabbit?"

"I rode on my two little white ones," she replied, daintily smoothing her skirts forward to cover her feet, as he threw himself down before her.

"The little white rabbits must be awfully tired."

"They are."

"Then they'll have to rest here a long time."

"Of course! For hours and hours!"

"Is this the first time the little white rabbits were ever in the woods?"

"They've been in a poor little cage ever since they were born. Didn't you know that?"

"And didn't they ever get tired of the cage before?"

"Oh, awfully tired."

"And now they are never going to be satisfied to stay in the cage again, are they?"

"No, never!"

"But what's going to become of them? Where are they going to stay?"

"Oh — *they'll* find a place — somewhere!"

"Don't you know there are a great many big dogs in the world that eat up little white rabbits?"

"Do they? How dreadful! And what becomes of these big dogs?"

"Oh — nothing! They just eat up some more!"

"Poor little rabbits! If mine were to see one of these dogs, how they would run!"

He laughed and lay on his back, watching her contentedly.

"What were you writing?" she asked with a gay threat some minutes later. "I saw you writing."

"A note to you. I thought you were not coming. I was going to send it to you."

"Then give it to me — it's mine!"

He drew out of his breast pocket a thick, old memorandum book and pulled off the strap.

It was a curious little book of his personal history. He had bought it upon his father's death, when he had come to the head of affairs, and begun to equip himself with things that gratified his idea of a young farmer's importance. About half of it was now taken up with such items as the price of agricultural implements, the number of bushels of grain to the acre, and the date of foals; but the last part was filled with other things.

In it were scribbled the names of a good many girls; on some of the pages a great many times the names of a few girls; on others the name of one girl had been written over and over. There were little confessions to some that had relieved his heart and delighted his eye with their air of confidential reality at the moment of writing them. Sometimes, also, when he had been riding in a buggy with a girl, to a church or to a picnic, and the way was long and the horse was tired, he had feigned to be far away from her, and had scribbled notes to her that became a thousand times more telling because of that intoxicating sham — because of that hopeless distance between them, while his shoulder lay against hers and their breaths mingled. He had done the same thing on long, black mohair sofas in parlours of a Sunday afternoon, availing himself of the dim light that came through the slits of the blinds and the shutters. And he had done the same thing in church with the help of a hymn-book, a handkerchief, or a palm-leaf fan — all the time keeping a pious eye on the preacher and looking remorseful about his sins.

He searched among the pages until he found

the note he had just written, and lay back again watching her.

It was her first love-letter. Imagine a fawn that for days has been wandering lost and athirst over rock and plain, but at last in some green woodland solitude sees the brink of a cold lake and one of the herd browsing near. More than water to thirst, or reunion with kind was this letter to Daphne. Among the things that he had written, he had set down his real disappointment that she had not met him, and he had added his determination to see her, no matter who forbade. Nevertheless, to him the scrap of paper meant something less than love. To her it was a sacred scroll, bidding her to enter the old, old earthly paradise.

As she finished reading it, she could not look at him. The flush of her own inward confession dyed her neck and face and brow. In her embarrassment her fingers began to turn over the leaves and her eyes to fall upon other names and other notes.

"Are these for me, also?" she asked simply.

He sprang up, turning a deep red.

"Give it here," he cried, trying to take the book from her.

"No!" cried Daphne, laughing. "You gave it to me to read!"

In a moment he was on his knees before her and had imprisoned her hand with the book in it. With the other he drew the book out and put it into his pocket. Then all at once the same unforeseen desire that had thrilled him that day in the meadow — the same unforeseen desire that had come over him as he braided the ring on her hand the day before — now rose in him with overmastering strength, and he held her hand.

"Don't, Hilary!" she said sweetly, with a little wince of pain. "Let me go. You hurt me!"

He caught her other hand.

"Hilary!" she cried again, with a deeper rebuke in her voice, falling backward against the tree and struggling to release her hands.

He tried to draw her to him with a low, caressing laugh.

"Hilary! *Hilary!*" she cried, resisting him

with a sudden terror of his advances, his rough tenderness, the torrent of his feelings. Then with one awful thought, and the strength it gave her, she struggled out of his arms to her feet, and stood supporting herself with one hand against the tree. He rose, and they confronted each other. The great solemn voices were sounding now: the divine bell was tolling now. Her face seemed cut from marble, and her eyes were full of fright and distress.

He looked at her, pale, without a word.

Then, as if realizing what she must do, she started homeward.

He sprang after her with a bitter cry to her.

She turned, her figure drawn quickly tense and her eyes filling with a calm, sad light. He could no more have spoken again, or taken one step, than he could have pulled up the oak-tree near him and offered it to her as a flower of apology. And so he stood watching her as she walked falteringly away from him until, gathering all her strength for one effort, she broke into a run, and tripped and fell, and got weakly up with one quick, frightened glance back at him, and then ran on.

For the first time in many years feeling that her home would be like heaven to reach, she fled through the woods.

When she had gained the house unnoticed, she passed as noiselessly as a shadow to her room, locked the door, and threw herself across the foot of her bed. Then reaching for a pillow, and drawing it with a tight clutch down over her face, she lay there.

The sun sank low, and its level rays coming through the little, green shutters kissed pityingly the shoes on her feet. One by one the sounds came on that mark the close of a summer day in the country: the calling of the cattle home and the bleat of calves at the milking; the jangling of trace-chains in the quiet, darkening air, as the workmen return from the fields to the barn; the cutting of oats for the horses; the last peaceful quarrels of the fowls going to roost in the trees about the yard; the play of the young negroes up at the woodpile; the shuffling of feet busy about the wash-basin on the porches below; and the loud beating of the biscuit and the grinding of coffee in the kitchen. Then the setting of the supper-table out on the porch, and the dragging of the chairs to their places; and across the big, white stones in the yard the careful tread of other feet, bringing the milk and butter from the cool spring-house.

At last her mother's voice — a meek, quavering treble — sounded at the foot of the stairs:

"Daphne, why don't you come to your supper?"

Ah! if she had had the right kind of a mother, all this would never have happened.

After an interval, bare feet rushed up the stairway, and impatient hands tried the door, and voices sounded through the keyhole.

"Daphne, you'd better come to your supper."

After another interval her father's voice, stern, inquiring, rose from the foot of the stair:

"Daphne?"

There was no answer.

"Daphne?"

There was no answer.

Then his heavy, awkward tread came up the steps, his toes kicking against the brass rods, and his hand shaking the knob violently.

"Daphne?"

She opened the door.

"What's the matter with you?" he said harshly and taking her by the arm led her over to the western window.

But when they reached it, she turned her face from the low light, and forgetting the past—all his coldness, all his unkindness, all the wrong—she threw her arms around his neck and hid her face on his bosom with a bitter cry:

"Oh, father! father! father! You are all that I have in the world."

Her voice pierced even him; and putting his arms around her, the hard, grisly man, for the first time in his life, strained her to his breast and cried out in broken tones over her head:

"My poor child! What has happened to you?"

XII

A CRYSTAL spring gurgled out of the limestone near the foot of the hill on which Daphne's home had been built by a pioneer forefather. The mouth of this spring had been enlarged and the earth dug away, allowing the water to spread over a flat basin of rock. From the lower edge of this it tinkled away through a mossy trough to the branch in the lot below. Over this basin of rock a spring-house had been built; large round stones placed here and there for the feet; and sunk in the dark, cold water were crocks and tins, keeping the milk and butter sweet in the fashion of times and manners now nearly gone. A foot-path ran down to the spring-house through the back yard and past an old orchard of apple and peach trees.

Toward dusk one evening, about two weeks later, Daphne had gone down, as often her custom was, to skim the milk for supper: the negro girl was soon to come for it.

But when she had entered the spring-house, she paused among the crocks and tins, lost in her thoughts. She had not had many thoughts in those two long, long weeks — poor Daphne! but the few she had never left her.

She was freshly dressed in a simple home frock of white. The ends of her long braids were tied together with a blue riband. A spray of heliotrope laid its fragrance on her round breast. She breathed the purity of a primrose that has just opened in the cool twilight grass. The gray-green light of the room, reflected from the white walls and from the moss of the rocks, threw upon her face a pallor that made its sadness very touching.

Seeing her standing thus, slender and still and white on the low, green stones as though poised on the leaves of the lotus, with only the voice of the tiny spring rippling on the silence as it struggled out of its caverns, the fancy forgot who she was and where she was and fell to dreaming of those faint, far shapes that in the youth of the world's imagination haunted the borderland of mystery and reality. What was she but a nymph of the fountain, brought by some late disaster to ponder the secrets of life and nature? Or drawing her comfort from the little spring, whose fate it was to fall clear from the skies; to run a little way over the earth now in light, now in darkness, gathering many stains; and at last to be drawn back home to the skies, clear once more?

She had stood thus only a few minutes when her ear caught the sound of feet on the stones outside. The next moment a figure darkened the doorway: she turned dreamily; it was Hilary.

He came down the few steps that led to the basin of rock and walked to the edge of it and stopped there, looking across at her with his face full of trouble.

She forgot her anger; forgot her humiliation; forgot the anguish in which she had lived since they had parted; forgot his boldness in daring to seek her in such a place and at such an hour, and the consequences to them both if he were discovered. She forgot everything but the joy of seeing him again which made itself felt beyond any power of help or hindrance.

But she grew as cold as though her feet were freezing to the rocks and her large, mournful, startled eyes put between him and her a distance that was not to be crossed.

"I have been trying to see you," he said, "trying every day — every day for two weeks. But you would not give me a chance: you have stayed at home. I understand! I am not blaming you! But I can't stand it any longer! If I had not seen you to-day, I was coming to the house to-morrow! I don't care!" he cried with a gesture of uncontrollable feeling as he saw a new look of fear on her face. "I was coming!" and as he spoke, for the first time there rang out in his voice his real love of her.

Nature had been having her way with him as an animal during these days of waiting; but something else had begun to have its way also — something that we satisfy ourselves by calling not earthly and of the body, but unearthly and of the soul — something that is not pursuit and enjoyment of another, but self-sacrifice for another's sake — that does not bring satiety but ever-growing dearness onward through youth and joy into old age and sorrow — that remains faithful when the one of two sits warm in the sun and the other lies cold in the shadow — that burns on and on as a faithful lonely flame in a worn-out broken lamp — and that asks, when everything else is over, for a life throughout eternity, spirit with spirit.

The change in him was unmistakable. She understood; and in a moment the whole past against him was blotted out.

He stepped upon the rocks toward her.

She stretched out one of her hands with a gesture of remonstrance.

"Go back!" she said faintly.

But he came on over and stood close before her and looked her imploringly in the eyes.

"I *can't* go away!" he said. "I understand how you feel! But you must try to understand how I feel, Daphne! Try to understand everything!"

"I can't talk to you here," she answered pleadingly. "If you will only go away! . . . They will be coming here in a minute . . . they will see you!"

"I am going back to the house with you," he replied stubbornly. "I am going to ask your father and mother for you . . . if you will only say . . ."

"No! No!" she cried. "It would only make it worse — worse for me! They have threatened me! . . . If I meet you again, they are going to send me away — to some school — for a year — two — three years! Will you go — for my sake?"

"They shall not send you away!" he replied. "It is not for them — it is for you to say."

"Oh, then, if you care for me don't stay here any longer."

"But when can I see you?"

"Only give me time to think."

"I will not go till you promise to meet me again! Will you come to the back of the pasture to-morrow?"

"I can't! I can't promise that."

"Don't you trust me now, Daphne?"

"Oh, yes, yes! But will you go?"

"Will you come to-morrow?"

"I will see you — somewhere — soon!"

"No!" he cried. "To-morrow! I must see you to-morrow! I'll wait for you. If you are not there, I am coming to the house."

"If you loved me," she said with a quick reproachful gesture, "you would go away now!"

He turned and went out.

XIII

She went to the rear of the pasture the next afternoon and found him waiting; and after that she met him there every few days, sometimes daily.

A pair of butterflies out of their countless kind had met on the meadows of life and, forgetting all others, were beginning to cling. The time was not far off when Nature would demand her crisis — that ever old, ever new miracle of the dust through which the perishable becomes the enduring, and the individual of a moment renews itself into a type for ages.

The crisis came on in beauty. The noon of summer now was nigh. Each day the great tawny sun became a more fierce and maddening lover of the earth, and flushed her more deeply, and awoke in her throes of responsive energy, until the whole land seemed to burn with colour and to faint in its own sweetness.

And this high aërial miracle of two floating spheres that swept all life along in the flow of its tide, caught the boy as a running sea catches a weed.

He began to lose energy and interest in his work. He would go out to the fields and forget everything, or not care; and throwing himself down in the shade of a tree, lie with his hat over his eyes until the dinner-horn sounded faint and clear, calling him home. When night fell he was restless and away, riding back late and slowly, not having spoken with any one. The mare's nervous ears often questioned his silent lips, and her eyes glanced uneasily backward at his figure, with its hands folded over the pommel of his saddle, and the moonlight shining on his face, serious and still. When he had turned her out, he sat for a long time smoking, and his mother's unseen fan often stirred the air softly about his face like the wing of a hovering bird. But he addressed few or no words to her; and at last with a wound at the change in him, but with no questions and with no suspicion of the cause, lingeringly she left him to his mood. Then his setter would creep nearer and lay her head heavily across his lap, uttering her reproachful whine. More than one sweet girl of the neighbourhood slipt out into her porch during the fragrant twilights of these days and waited for the sound of a front gate being opened; but he did not come. And in a private street of the town not far away a richly furnished house, with lighted windows kept well curtained and closed, also missed him greatly and persistently.

All women to him had become Daphne in the woods.

At first he had urged her to let him speak to her father and mother and end the secrecy, but she had counselled that this would be worse than cruelty to her; they disliked him bitterly; she was a child. *He* was a child also, she added; but the look with which she said this was not the look that one child gives another. For both reasons her father would separate them at once; and at the mere thought of her separation from him she betrayed how her life now clung to his. He reflected — for his own part — upon the folly of marrying at his age, with no roof of his own to shelter her, and with his mother's certain anger and probable refusal to receive them even for a while into her home.

Thus they continued to meet, and he realized that she did not understand the constantly increasing danger.

For she had greatly changed. At the opening of June, but a few weeks before, she had been of a fretful and rebellious temper, dissatisfied with her surroundings, without a tie in life that kept her in constant activity, and therefore in constant rest. But under that rapid growth which some women undergo when the revelation of Nature has fallen upon them for the first time, and with the explanation it gives of so many things, all her vague yearnings had taken rigid order or sunk into nothingness around this single passion. She, too, had behind her generations of immoral forefathers, each of whom in weakening the moral fibre of his own nature had helped to weaken hers. It was along the edge of the sad immemorial harvests sown by them that her wayward feet were straying.

And now the thought preyed ceaselessly upon him of how another man in his place might use his advantage.

But it aroused in him, at least, the greater care that his own power over her should become her defender. He did not forget that she had been drawn into this false situation by his urgency; and whatever else he may not have had, he had the spirit of fair play. Her absolute trust of him alone would have put him upon his honour, even had not the first impulse of his love been to draw about her the circle of sacredness. Perhaps something in his dissolute past had already taught him that a man's love for a woman is bound up with his knowledge — or at least his belief — of her purity.

There were days when he scarcely dared see her; and not once had he so much as touched her hands, except at meeting and at parting.

At times he was grave and silent, as though he were revolving some plan for them in the knowledge of which he allowed her no share; at other times — indeed always — he struck her as being secretly troubled. If she sought to question him, he was rude and cross with her. She misunderstood the change in him, and was deeply wounded; and her old wretched doubts of him returned. Was this the beginning of coldness and withdrawal? Did he care for her after all? No woman feels sure in such a case — and the case has many forms in life — what it is that has attracted a man, or how long and at what a price she can hold him.

Thus her love rose in her like a spring that must overflow in the end, and he lay beside the spring with a parched tongue.

One afternoon as he was riding along that side of his farm, he hitched his mare and walked across to the spot where they were in the habit of meeting. Once she had asked him whether he ever came to it when she was not there, and he had said that he often felt like coming.

She was there already. The afternoon before they had shifted their position under the trees to avoid the sun, and had gone to a fresh place in the cool grass. When they had risen, she had laughed at the print of his figure.

She lay in this print of his figure now, with her face buried in her hands. Something in her attitude made him feel sure that she was praying. He left the place quickly, noiselessly, with a new awe of her.

That night as he sat alone on the porch, his thoughts returned to this scene. What impulse had drawn her to the place? And of what could she be praying? Was the struggle going on in her nature, as in his, the same struggle?

Over the tree-tops the stars of the southern summer night were glowing with chaste fire. The flowers about the yard were releasing their last fragrance to the night; and from their hiding-places under the leaves, beneath the grass, in the crevices of the roof and the walls, everywhere, the butterflies of the earth's shadow with wings of silver and breasts of snow were hurrying to the blossoms, circling about their loves, pursuing and meeting each other in the languorous darkness.

He had been of their roving kind — using their freedom, lacking their innocence — a seeker of the fast-fading buds of the night.

Nature had never made him of the highest or for the highest, and he had already fallen a good deal lower than he was made; but of late the linking of his life to a pure one, in duty and in desire, had helped him in his struggle to do what was right. The recollection of the scene of to-day touched him most deeply, and perhaps during these moments he realized as far as was possible to him now, that the happiness of a man's life lies and must always lie where a woman's lies.

But on the shifting sands of a false past and with hands little fitted for the work, he was making his first sincere but blundering effort to rear a barrier of a moral resistance as the safeguard of two lives. And far out on the deeps of life Nature, like a great burying wave, was rolling shoreward toward him.

XIV

Lovely June had gone and nearly all July. It was Saturday and for an hour or more the shadows of things had been lengthening eastward.

A great circus had come to town that day. From early morning a band of white dust, beginning on the green horizon at the north and disappearing on the green horizon at the south, had hung over the turnpike, marking the passage of vehicles and horsemen. At every station the train had taken on gaily dressed, merry people.

Quiet as if Sunday rest had fallen upon the fields. A plough lay at the end of a furrow, the earth still undried upon the mole, the gear pitched among the weeds in the fence corner, the horses scarce done drinking at the pond in the woods and wearing the sweat mark of the collar on their necks. A yoke of oxen stood resting under a mighty elm, the loaded wagon left in the far-away fields, beside the unfinished wheat stack. For miles in every direction hardly a voice or a human presence on the landscape, except perhaps the slumberous singing of an old negro at work with a loving hoe among the watermelon vines or the sweet potatoes.

Upon many of the homesteads a quiet greater still — some closed, door and shutter, and not a soul remaining. Here a barn door had been left unbolted, so that the calves had gotten in and were tearing the yellow heads of the new oats; there a garden gate unlatched, and the fowls were scratching up the late peas and sinking their bills into the red tomatoes. In the cabin door of one farm-house under her gourd-vines and sunflowers, a granny might have been sitting, her fillet of white wool silvering in the sunbeams between her ebon brow and scarlet turban, her clawlike finger on the bowl of her pipe, a babe asleep across her knees. On the porch at another house, in the shadow of the Catawba grape-vines, an old farmer dozed solitary in his sock feet and unbuttoned waistcoat; or — he having passed away — his wife, with her Bible in her lap and heavy spectacles on her dim eyes, sat softly rocking, and knitting, and praying, soon to be with him in the world of eternal youth.

Upon the midsummer woods most of all lay brooding stillness and subtle relaxing heat. In the depths of one the moo of a restless heifer broke at intervals upon the ear like a faint, far bell of distress. The squirrel hid asleep. The cuckoo barely lilted in silky flight among the trees. The mourning moth lay on the thistle with flattened wings as still as death. The blue snake-doctor had dropped on the brink of the green pool like a lost jewel. Amid such silence in a forest, the imagination takes on the belief that all things in Nature understand and are waiting for some one to come — for something to happen that they will all feel.

Daphne glided like a swift, noiseless shadow into the woods.

It was partly by reason of her doubt of him that she had arranged their meeting for this afternoon. He had been telling her that he was going to the circus; and she had jealously watched the eagerness with which he looked forward to that pleasure. He had been keenly disappointed therefore when she had named this day and he had begged her to set another; but she had refused, and at last he had said that this day it should be.

To avoid suspicion, he was to drive to town in the morning, let himself be seen on the streets by the people from the neighbourhood, and allow it to be taken for granted that he was going to the circus. He was to come out by another turnpike, drive across through a lane, and hitch his buggy somewhere near the woods. Daphne was to remain at home with her grandmother — the country would be deserted — they would have the whole afternoon to themselves.

But when she now reached the edge of the pawpaw thicket and peeped through the branches, there was no one sitting at the foot of the ash-tree. She stepped anxiously into the open space and looked about her. With a sweet smile of discovery she ran to the tree and peeped behind. Then she stood with her hand against it, overcome with disappointment. But he might be hiding somewhere near.

"Hilary!" she cried.

Her voice was so faint that it could have penetrated only a few yards. Amid the deep silence of the woods it terrified her as though it could be heard back at the house. But there was something worse now than even the fear of being heard.

"Hilary!" she cried more loudly. Of all those little appeals that the women send out for the men in such cases — for the men who do not intend to come — none could ever have been more distressing.

A ground-squirrel that had been watching her from between two fence rails darted with a shriek into his hole. It gave her a great start, and out of sheer weakness she sat down. Then she bent her ear, listening. Only the bell-like moo in her father's pasture.

The world was suddenly to Daphne as if sackcloth had been drawn over the sun.

The temptation to stay in town had been too great: he was not coming. He knew that she would be there, waiting; but that was nothing to him. He was tired of her, and had deserted her, as she had always known that he would. She drew her knees up and laid her sick, white face over on them.

Then there was the sound of feet hurrying nearer, and the snapping of dried twigs under the grass; then the breaking of a rail on the fence, as a heavy weight was thrown recklessly upon it; and then he hurried round into the open space, and when he saw her, stopped short, with his hat in his hand and the worried expression on his face vanishing as though he had stepped from shadow into sunlight.

In an instant she noticed — as in their unlike ways women do — little changes in his appearance which left him more attractive in her rustic eyes: he had on a new suit of clothes which made him look cool and sweet; he had had his hair cut and was freshly shaved, so that his face wore the freshness of a child's that still has the wholesome fragrance of the bath upon it.

The happiness of knowing that she had wronged him — that he had given up everything for the sake of coming back to her — that he was hers absolutely — wrought the betrayal of Daphne's self-control. She was taken off her guard. Her love swept her on like a flood. With a cry of gratitude and delight she ran to him, but checked herself, and merely caught his hand and kissed it again and again, and pressed it to her bosom, and laid her cheek down on it and held it there, closing her eyes to hide her tears.

And this in her was so sudden and so maddening to him that, taken off his guard also — his long self-restraint swept away — with a low answering cry he threw his arms around her and drew her form in against his. Then, bending her slowly backward, his face close over her face, he pressed his lips to hers.

The young trust themselves alone with Nature, who cares only for life and nothing for the higher things that make life worth the living. To them who understand her deadly approaches she can come least near with the power to harm. When her low storm threatens, they can rise to higher strongholds, perhaps to the great calm crags of spiritual retreat, and look down with pity upon her havoc in the plain. But the young, who have not learned and do not suspect, these from the creation of the world she has been engulfing as those who once walked between walls of water.

How still the woods were all around! How still the trees were overhead. For centuries their roots, their boughs and buds and heart fibres, had witnessed the love histories of the irresponsible little creatures of earth and air that had come and gone, countless and forgotten, like their own leaves. Never had Nature driven to them such an earthly pair, two ephemera of immortal destinies.

How still the woods were, except that not far away, in Hilary's pasture, a wild, dangerous bull, whose blood was raging, paused once as he roved nearer and listened, his head in the air; then with a deep answering roar came hurrying on: a vast bulk with noble arching neck covered with red curls; red curls about the base of his crescent horns; a central sun of white curls between his sullen, majestic eyes; his head now swung low; the snowy fringes of his tail rippling far behind across the grass and weeds.

Straight on toward the still trees he moved, with the lash of his feet through the grass, and the snapping of vines across his resistless brows — straight on toward a panel of the fence where the briers were short and the top rail broken. The pause of an instant there; then his awful weight was lifted, and came crushing down.

With a cry of alarm Hilary sprang up and stood between him and Daphne. But the great glad beast, looking neither to the right nor to the left, and with one announcing roar, swept past them.

When Hilary turned, Daphne had risen and gone. She had sunk on the grass some yards away, and she had hidden her face in her hands and was crying bitterly.

He did not go to her. He did not know what to do, or what he was doing. He walked mechanically around to the broken panel and stood looking over into his pasture, seeing everything, and seeing nothing.

He was like a traveller who has passed from the radiance of moonlight into the blackness of a tempest and been blinded by a red flame in his face; so that for a moment he does not feel his feet under him, or know his road, but stands with the crash of the heavens in his ears, and a sense of his helplessness amid the forces of Nature that are freeing themselves without any concern for his life or his death. But even while he stands thus — perhaps the next minute — a few rays may struggle down into the pit of darkness, recalling him to his path and to what reigns on above the storm.

He came around from behind the briers and hurried across the open space to where Daphne sat; and, dropping on one knee before her, he began to speak to her. He had the air of a man who has thrown away everything for the sake of one only. At first she did not hear or heed; later she listened. Then for a few minutes longer they spoke together passionately, he pleading, she refusing; after which he got up and walked to and fro, while she buried her face in her hands again. Then he glanced at his watch, and with an exclamation returned to her.

"There's only a little time left, Daphne!" he said imploringly. "We barely have time before the train passes. We can arrange everything on the way to the station. There is no one to stop us. Will you go with me?"

She did not answer.

He got down on his knee again and laid his hand tenderly on her head and urged her yet another time:

"We can get to Aberdeen to-night. . . . We can be married to-night. . . . Won't you go with me, Daphne?"

Still she did not answer. So that he rose and stood looking down upon her in silence. His one thought was the danger they had just escaped, and the one duty before him, as he saw it now, was clear as noonday. When he spoke again, it was with a sudden wrench of nature.

"Then, Daphne, I am going to tell you good-by — now!"

She sprang up and came close, and looked him piercingly in the eyes.

"What do you mean?" she said.

"I mean," he answered, "that you must go with me, and marry me now, or we must not meet in this way any more."

"Oh!" she cried, clasping her hands to her heart and looking at him piteously.

"Daphne," he cried, "your father will never consent. . . . If we are ever to marry, we'll have to go in this way. But if you will not go," he added with a forced harshness that he had never used to her before, "then — go home."

She stood, her tears arrested, her lips quivering, her eyes searching his face miserably.

"You mean," she asked at length, slowly, "that — you — will — not — meet — me — here — any — more?"

"No."

She closed her eyes, and a shiver passed through her as though his words had cut her like a lance. Then she came a step nearer to him, with a fear in her eyes that was awful to see; and in the same slow way she asked again:

"You — mean — that — you — will — not — meet — me — *anywhere* — *any* — *more* ?"

"No!" he cried again with blind impetuosity and the same forced harshness.

There was no playground in the summer woods for them now but a bare foothold on a steep mountain rock; the right and the wrong of life and death yawned near them.

"Marry me now!" he cried for the last time and with a warning.

She stood bending slightly toward him, looking beyond him into the future if she yielded. She foresaw the unforgiveness of her father and mother, which would last through life; the anger of his mother, whom she dreaded; the long distance to be travelled, and the risk of their being stopped on the way; the river to be crossed; the uncertainty of getting the marriage ceremony performed that night, and the necessity of her being left alone with him in a strange place. To this last thought was linked a new fear of herself and of him that had been aroused during the last hour; for Nature had stolen treacherously nigh them both, as is her sad, sad wont with her human children. And with this fear now came again the old torturing doubts of him. He was no longer even a member of the church, and to her mind this was the last thing that made her fear that he might not do what was right.

The moments were flying and he did not understand her silence.

"I thought you loved me!" he cried angrily, with a sting in his tone and his first distrust of her.

She turned upon him one look of reproach beyond words.

And then, as if this doubt of her drove her on, she came quickly and laid her hands on his shoulders.

"Promise me if I go with you, Hilary," she said very rapidly and incoherently, "promise me if I go with you — no, give me your word of honour! — no, swear to me! — swear by the name of your mother, who hates me! — swear before God! — that you will not — that you will — "

She took her hands from his shoulders and folded them over his forehead, and pressed his face back and gazed into his eyes as her tears rained down her face.

" — that you will be — *true* — to me!"

If she had been confronted with the women who have asked that pledge and with the men who have broken it!

He gave her a look of surprise.

"There is no need for me to promise," he exclaimed, beside himself with joy. "Only let us make haste. It is almost too late!" and he would have led her away.

She recoiled with a cry of astonishment. He turned back to her speechless. She made one little gesture with her hand:

"Promise — swear!"

"You love me and do not trust me?" he asked roughly. As if there are not always in the world women who love men well enough to die for them and doubt them enough to kill them.

"Will you promise? Will you swear?"

"You have no right to ask it," he cried hotly, aroused to resist her with all his strength. For no matter what such a man's past may have been, he wishes to be taken by the woman he loves as he takes her.

"You ask all this of me?" she replied, "and you are not willing to give me any pledge — any?"

"If you could not trust me without one, what would it be worth if I gave it?" he exclaimed more passionately still.

Her hands dropped at her sides, then with another slight gesture of dismissal she turned homeward, saying faintly:

"I will not go with you!"

He sprang before her.

"Daphne," he cried, breaking completely down, "I will promise! I will promise you anything!"

She searched his face sorrowfully and then gave him her hand.

"Ah, but you should have promised at first," she said with great gentleness, and her tears flowed again.

"If we are to go, we must be going!" he implored.

"Yes! if we are to go, we must be going," she answered sadly; and then realizing that the last moment of her girlhood had come, that love was leading her on into the unknown, that every other human tie was falling away from her, and that she might be tempted beyond her strength, with a sudden turning to the fortress of her religion, she sank upon her knees and pulled him down before her.

"Here, on your knees," she said, shaken by her sobs, "give me your solemn oath, Hilary — before God, who sees us and will judge us for what we do — that wherever we are together — whatever may happen to us — you will be *true* to me . . . *true* to me . . . *true* to me!"

"I swear!" he said, his eyes filling, "God helping me, I will be true to you!"

XV

THE broad, lofty plateau of Middle Kentucky where the rich farm lands lie sinks slowly westward to the Ohio. There the great tawny river throws a caressing arm around the coming hills, dividing the South from the North.

At a certain point on the river bank these verdurous hills jut out against the southern sky like the fragments of enormous emeralds. Along the base of them stretches the old town of Maysville. Opposite, on the Ohio side, lies the old village of Aberdeen — hardly more than a quiet hamlet. A ferry plies between.

Here in early days was a great historic crossing, a pathway of primeval travel, a waterway of southward moving civilization, a gateway of northwestern war; and here for three-quarters of a century, until a few years ago, the fleeing couples of Kentucky escaped from the

State to be married by the squires on the other side.

It was late that night. The spirit of the infinite and the divine seemed to brood throughout the universe. In Nature reigned only the law of beauty and of peace.

The moon hung on the violet walls of the sky like a broken shield of beaten gold — hung there as if to be at rest from the clangour of arms forevermore. The stars burned as great cathedral tapers, freshly lighted for some chaste processional of the soul. The air, blowing from the south through the rifts in the emerald hills, brought with it the thoughts of quiet meadows far away, of noiseless hemp and corn, of cattle drowsing in the deep, cool grass near some silvering flake of water. The river rolled on in curves of light, unbroken by keel or oar, the ferry-man asleep. Only some glowing window in the town betrayed the watchful or the sleepless; and once in a dark alley the voices of a man and a woman parting in a doorway — the locking of the door, and the sounds of his feet hurrying unsteadily away — jarred rudely upon the thought that all things were at rest under the wing of darkness and in the beauty of holiness.

Suddenly a skiff shot out from the Kentucky bank a little way above the town and started in a slanting line across the river. In the stern sat two figures.

As the boat passed out into the mighty current, whether filled with the fear of it and of what was coming, or chilled by the cooler wind that blew on her — she had on a thin dress and had no wrap — the girl shivered. The boy took off his coat and, folding it about her shoulders, drew it softly across her bosom and buttoned it under her throat.

"You must not get cold," he said, bending over her. She looked up at him gratefully.

"Don't take off your coat," she said. "You will catch cold. Please don't — for my sake."

"Oh, I'm warm," he replied carelessly.

All the afternoon, from the moment of their starting, the new reverence with which he treated her put her in new awe of him. As she nestled into the coat and the warmth of his body passed into hers, she slipped one of her hands down between his burning palms.

Far out in the stream the powerful young fellow at the oars addressed them, being tired of the silence.

"You're not the first couple I've taken over to-day. I rowed one over just after sundown. We hadn't more than shoved off when her father was down on them. He walked quietly down to the edge of the river and levelled his shot-gun and said: 'Come back!' But the young fellow in the boat, he moved away from his girl, and then he said to me just as quietly: 'You go on!'"

When the boat had been run ashore and they had gotten out, he stepped up to Hilary, for whom he had conceived a liking.

"I reckon you'll need me for a witness," he said.

"Witness! Do we have to have witnesses?"

"Of course."

"How many?"

"Two."

"Do you know where I can get another?"

"Maybe I can pick up one as we go along. Maybe we can get one at the hotel next door to the squire's."

Their voices were as low and grave as though they had been arranging the details of a military execution. The three walked through the moonlit village in silence. There was not a sound anywhere. On the farther edge of it in a street leading back in the country, they stopped before a large two-story house. Old maple-trees stood in front of it on the sidewalk, covering it now with shifting light and shadow. On one side was a yard and in the yard stood old apple-trees. From under one of the apple-trees came the low sound of a fife.

"That's the squire," said the oarsman. "He is used to being up at all hours of the night. Wait here."

He entered the yard gate. Soon the sound of the fife ceased. Then followed the sound of feet passing into the house from a back porch; then the noise of feet inside; and then the front door was opened, and in the doorway, holding a lamp high over his head, stood a lean, wrinkled, old man with short white hair, heavy, circling eyebrows over vivacious, sunken eyes, and the general demeanour of a firm and polite Frenchman.

"Come in," he said simply.

They walked into the parlour. He went back into the hall, with a nod to Hilary.

"The fee is five dollars," he said.

Hilary thrust his hand into his pocket and drew out two dollars and some change.

"I didn't know I was coming. This is all I have. But I can send it."

The squire took the two dollars from his palm and reëntered the parlour.

"Are you ready?" he said.

The oarsman had come in, bringing with him the keeper of the hotel. Hilary walked over to where Daphne sat on a chair holding her hat and her handkerchief in her hand. He took her by the other hand and drew it inside his arm.

The squire stepped before them. He spoke in the tone in which a witness is sworn in a court-room.

"Marriage is a solemn ordinance, instituted by an all-wise Being for the happiness of man and woman. It is a solemn pledge, or contract, entered into by the parties, which is to continue through life.

"Join your hands.

"Each of you do solemnly promise that you will love, honour, and obey each other as a dutiful husband and wife; and, forsaking all others, cleave to each other alone until it shall please Almighty God to separate you by death. To this do you both agree?"

There was silence. Each waited for the other to speak.

"To this do you both agree?" repeated the squire sharply.

Hilary shifted his weight heavily from one foot to the other.

"I do!" he said, in a thick, nervous tone.

"I do!" said Daphne, in a low, trembling voice, with an effort to give some dignity to her vow, but with a pathetic sense also of how alone she was among those strange men and of how unlike all this was to a wedding.

"In the presence of Almighty God and these witnesses present, by authority vested in me, I now pronounce you husband and wife."

The hotel-keeper stepped forward.

"Your room will be ready when you come over," he said, and went out.

The oarsman, who had not been able to keep his eyes from Daphne's face since they had come into the light of the room, stepped forward and shook hands with rough warmth.

"Partner!" he said to Hilary, "I'll change boats with you!"

Then he, too, went out: nothing had been said about paying him.

The squire had opened a writing-desk of a pattern ancient and now little seen: with quaint drawers and upright shelves, and many pigeon-holes. He had taken his seat before this, and was unrolling a sheet of paper nearly covered with closely written names. Other sheets and numerous little rolls of paper of a few inches square — some of them yellow and crumpled and covered with dust, and all of them filled with names — bulged from the pigeon-holes, and were crammed away between the upright shelves.

There they were — the rolls of the secret marriages of the people of Kentucky. Thousands upon thousands of couples. Many of them not much more than children, sometimes one couple a day, sometimes three or four. A long, gay pageant: some less gay than others, being desperately pursued; some less gay, not being guiltless; some most sorrowfully bent upon the office of having the marriage performed and the date of it set back for the sake of the poor little life soon to appear in the world. In quick succession the fugitives trod upon each other when Nature had begun to inflame the earth in the mornings of May and June; or in the languishing noons of autumn, during the season of rural fairs; or later still, when the wine was ready to burst the grape, and when the first fire on the hearth stirred in the blood the desire of human warmth during the long winter nights.

If Daphne had but known, hidden away on

one of those yellow sheets were the names of her own father and mother.

"Your names and ages," said the squire. "And where do you live?"

"Hilary ——, aged nineteen, Bourbon County, Kentucky."

"Daphne ——, aged seventeen, Fayette County, Kentucky."

The squire wrote down the words, added the date and the amount of the fee, and laid a blotter on what he had written. Then rising, he led the way to the front door.

"Good-night!" he said politely, and turned the key on them.

They stood as in a dream under the shadows of the old maples and looked around them. A light fell out upon the sidewalk from a door of the house adjoining, and a man was waiting on the steps.

"This way," he said.

They went over and followed him into the parlour.

"Have you had any supper?" he asked.

"We've had supper," said Hilary.

"Can I do anything for you?" He looked from one to the other. Hilary glanced covertly at Daphne.

"No!" she said quickly, and turned away from both of them.

"You'll find your room at the head of the stairs, when you get ready to go up," he said. "Take this lamp with you. Goodnight."

He went out, but came back and thrust in his head.

"*You* can lock the front door," he said to Hilary, significantly.

It was all over now — the life of peril and unrest from which they had barely escaped — with its tossing nights, its wistful, heartsore days, its ungovernable yearnings.

An awkward, embarrassed silence fell upon them the moment they were left alone. Daphne turned to a picture of the squire, that hung over the mantelpiece. From that she passed to a window, opening upon the rear of the yard, and stood for a little while, looking out tremblingly at the grass and the trees, silvered with moonlight. Then she sank upon a small, stiff chair, and dropping her eyes on her lap, began passing her fingers slowly, mechanically, around her handkerchief, going from corner to corner, corner to corner.

Across the room Hilary had sat down by the table, on which stood the small dim lamp, and had picked up the photograph album. The pictures ran: grandfather, grandmother; father, mother; then the children from the oldest down to the latest born. There was a portrait of a young mother clasping an infant triumphantly to her breast. There was another of a rustic young husband with his bride on his arm, and with a smile on his face that was like a challenge to the beholder to do anything better in life than that — or be anything better himself, if he could. Then came relatives and friends — with a few places at the back of the album for scattering and less valued acquaintances.

He went through them all from beginning to end, confusedly, never once lifting his eyes.

His hand was shaking, his face was flushed, and his tongue was palsied.

The hour had come to him when, of all that can ever come to man, he feels that he must begin a new life and when he would like to begin it as one newly born; when his old past rises against him; when, if there is anything decent and manly surviving in him still, he is overwhelmed with some sense of the awful gift that love has brought into his unworthy life, — a pure woman.

The great heights were never to be for Hilary. His ancestors, his companions, Nature, his own temperament and limitations, had appointed him his poor rough place far lower down; but if there ever descended upon him any rays of that divine light of the spirit which also rests upon such a union; if there ever reached him any fresh vision of the real manliness of what is right; these intimations from the wisdom of everlasting law, from the perpetuity of the species, and from the growing, triumphing movement of the world, conquered him and crushed him now.

The album slipped from his hands to the table. He started, and stole a look at her.

The moonlight, streaming through the window, rested upon her bare, lovely head, and upon one side of her face. He could see how white it was, how frightened, how appealing in its loneliness: a child — his wife — awaiting his will — submissive.

A new feeling of protecting tenderness rose in him for her; and with a quick, deep breath he started up and went over, and took both her hands softly in his and stood before her, looking reverently down at her.

"Will you go up now, Daphne?" he said, in a low tone. "It is so late, and you must sleep."

Her head dropped forward a little lower.

"Go, dearest," and his hands gathered themselves about hers with the strong, true pressure of a promise.

She lifted her face to him.

"You go with me," she whispered. "I'm afraid."

He turned to the lamp solemnly, and led the way. When he reached the door, he glanced back. She sat still in the chair.

"Come on," he said, with something in his voice that drew her irresistibly to him.

She rose and began to follow. But when she reached the foot of the stair, she stopped, faint and trembling, and watched him as he went slowly up. How heavy his tread was, how large his limbs were, how broad his back looked with the lamplight close in front of it! There was a pitiful fear of him in her eyes, and her bosom rose and fell with her quivering breath.

But at last she was happy and at peace: he was hers. The old, troublesome, uncertain life with him in the meadows, now so far away, at the picnic, in the pasture, was at an end. Girlhood, too, was at an end now; and with a certain new pity of herself she recalled the day when, careless and free, she had walked home across the fields in the warmth of early June, and had paused to hear him singing in the corn.

He reached the top of the stairs and, turning, raised the lamp above his head. But when he looked down and saw her at the bottom, he came back down the stairs and put his arm closely around her and they went up together.

THE END

www.ingramcontent.com/pod-product-compliance
Lightning Source LLC
Chambersburg PA
CBHW020256170426
43202CB00008B/397